Law and Licensing
A concise guide for shotgun and rifle owners
by Bill Harriman

The British Association for Shooting & Conservation

Quiller

Copyright © 2016 Bill Harriman

First published in the UK in 2016
by Quiller, an imprint of Amberley Publishing Ltd

Second edition 2022

British Library Cataloguing-in-Publication Data
A catalogue record for this book is available from the British Library

ISBN 978 1 84689 280 6 (paperback)
ISBN 978 1 84689 282 0 (ebook)

The right of Bill Harriman to be identified as the author of this work has been asserted in accordance with the Copyright, Design and Patent Act 1988.

The information in this book is true and complete to the best of our knowledge. All recommendations are made without any guarantee on the part of the Publisher, who also disclaims any liability incurred in connection with the use of this data or specific details.

All rights reserved. No part of this book may be reproduced or transmitted in any form or by any means, electronic or mechanical including photocopying, recording or by any information storage and retrieval system, without permission from the Publisher in writing.

Printed in the UK

Quiller
An imprint of Amberley Publishing Ltd
The Hill, Merrywalks, Stroud, GL5 4EP
Tel: 01453 847 800
E-mail: info@quillerbooks.com
Website: www.quillerpublishing.com

Contents

The Author	4
Acknowledgements	4
Introduction	5
Applying for a certificate	7
Dealing with the police	10
Firearms Licensing: Statutory Guidance for Chief Officers of Police	11
Unannounced visits	19
Suitability reviews	20
Residency qualifications	22
Travelling with guns	32
Guns in overnight accommodation	33
Shooting near buildings, roads, etc.	36
Falling shot	37
Replacement certificates	39
Temporary permits	39
Carrying your certificate	41
Guns in public	42
Shooting without certificates	44
Drink driving	47
Armed trespass	49
Sound moderators	50
Young people and firearms licensing	52
Young people and shotgun certificates	53
How the licensing process should work	54
Young people and firearms	57
Young people and shotguns	58
Age limits for possessing firearms and shotguns	59
Fees for certificates	60
Cartridges with expanding missiles (bullets)	61
Ballistic minima values for shooting deer	62
Pistols for humane despatch	64
Antique firearms	66
Prohibited persons	73
Air weapons	74
Relevant component parts of guns	76
Crown Court appeals	78
What constitutes a public place?	79
The Royal Society for the Prevention of Cruelty to Animals	80
Knives	81
Social media and firearm licensing	83
Transfer of firearms	85
The 72-hour rule	86
Dual ownership of firearms and shotguns	87
Shotgun cartridges	88
Guns and violence	88
Index	90

The Author

Bill Harriman is BASC's Director of Firearms, having joined the staff in 1991. Prior to that he worked in Birmingham for a firm of auctioneers specialising in guns, arms and armour. From 1974 to 1991, he served in the TA (Royal Artillery and Royal Yeomanry), retiring with the rank of Captain.

He has been one of a team of arms and militaria specialists for the BBC TV programme, *Antiques Roadshow* since 1985. He is also a Fellow of the Society of Antiquaries of London and an honorary historical advisor to the Royal Armouries. He is also President of the Muzzle Loaders Association of Great Britain.

He is a professional member of the Chartered Society for Forensic Science and routinely gives evidence in court about ballistic issues.

Bill collects infantry rifles (1830–1918), their ammunition and accessories. He also enjoys rough shooting, particularly with a muzzle loader. Outside of shooting, Bill enjoys real ale, opera, painting model soldiers and playing snooker in his club in Chester. He lives in North Wales, is married to Janet and has two adult daughters, Annabel and Caroline.

Acknowledgements

Peter Glenser QC, barrister at law for his legal input.

BASC's Firearms Team for its constant support and forum for lively debate on legal issues.

Introduction

A great deal of change has happened to firearms licensing law since the first edition of this book was published in 2016.
We have seen:

- The government issue statutory guidance to chief officers of police in an attempt to achieve administrative consistency in the firearms licensing process.

- A universal requirement for independent medical verification of certificate applications.

- A change to the law in the way that non-certificate holders can borrow shotguns and rifles.

- The complete revision of the law relating to antique firearms, including a definition of what constitutes an antique firearm in law.

- The introduction of a new concept in the definitions section of the Firearms Act 1968, that of the 'relevant component parts' of a firearm and their definition.

- The repeal of the prohibition on rifle cartridges loaded with expanding bullets.

- An automatic eight-week extension to expired certificate life providing application to renew it was made eight weeks prior to expiry.

This new edition highlights these areas of change and describes them in detail. That said, firearms law still remains complicated and difficult to understand. It is also in need of urgent codification.

This edition is also being published some two years after the government's restrictions made at the height of the Covid-19 pandemic. These caused chaos by imposing additional burdens on an already broken and shambolic system. Lengthy delays are now endemic and early application to renew is vital.

The single incident mass killings perpetrated by Jake Davison at Keyham in August 2021 cast yet another shadow over firearms licensing by heightening the pre-existent risk-averse culture within police firearms licensing circles. The inquests into the deceased have yet to be heard and the report into the incident by the Independent Office for Police Conduct will not be published until they conclude. Yet there is already talk of tightening up firearms law even though the facts of this dreadful incident have yet to be fully established. Any such changes must be evidence led, if the old adage of 'Hard cases make bad law' is to be avoided.

Bill Harriman
Marford
March 2022

Applying for a certificate

In making any application to the police for a firearm or shotgun certificate, it is a good idea to have the mindset that you, as a citizen of Great Britain, enjoy a qualified right to possess a firearm. Contrary to what some politicians, officials and police officers may imagine, firearms ownership for lawful purposes is not a privilege. I would describe it as a qualified right or reasonable expectation.

The British Association for Shooting and Conservation (BASC) made a submission to the Home Affairs Committee in 2010 to set this out in some detail:

'BASC does not agree with the proposition that the ownership of firearms for legitimate purposes by suitable persons is a privilege. We assert that it is a right, albeit one which is conditional of certain legally defined criteria being satisfied. The language at Section 27(1) of the 1968 Act sustains this: "*A firearm certificate shall be granted...*" and Section 28(1) "*...a shotgun certificate shall be granted...*" The term "*shall*" is used rather than "*may*", as is the case in Northern Ireland where the Chief Officer has absolute discretion. The use of the mandatory word "shall" is no historical accident and comes from the recommendations of the Blackwell Committee of 1919.'

Firearms law serves two functions: the prevention of illegal firearm use in crime and the preservation of public safety. It is also enabling legislation that allows people who want to own guns for legitimate purposes to do so via the mechanism of the licensing regime run by the police service. In addition firearms law specifies what a person may not do with a gun. There is an overarching concept in English law called *'freedom under the law'*. Law does not allow people to do things; rather it prevents them from doing things which are generally regarded as being harmful to society at large. Essentially, any activity is permitted unless the law explicitly says that it is not.

When you apply for a certificate it should be assumed by the police that your application is made for bona fide reasons for owning a gun, for example, wildfowling, clay pigeon shooting, target shooting, hunting deer or collecting. It is not the role of the police to dissuade you from possessing guns, nor to restrict different types of firearm from being lawfully acquired. Each case must be taken on its merits with the overarching view that in licensing an individual to possess guns public safety needs to be preserved. There is no place for a personal agenda. Each case needs to be risk-assessed and all the relevant issues considered. In risk-assessing a case, risk can never be eliminated entirely, merely minimised. A reasonable test would be: 'Is there any readily foreseeable harm in giving this person unfettered access to a gun?'

In the case of a firearm certificate (FAC) the applicant must prove to the police that he has 'good reason' for each and every firearm for which he is applying (Section 27(1)(b) Firearms Act 1968). The onus is on the applicant to do this. There is a whole section on 'good reason' in chapter 12 of the *Guide on Firearms Licensing Law* published by the Home Office, which is well worth a read. The Guide can be downloaded from the Government's website at www.gov.uk/government/publications. Chapter 12 covers most eventualities, especially the use of sporting rifles for hunting and pest control. There is no legal definition of 'good reason' as it must be construed according to normal usage using what is called the 'plain meaning rule'. What is clear, is that 'good reason' must be substantial, i.e. have substance and not be a matter of fancy or momentary whim. It is down to the applicant to prove to the police that he has 'good reason', i.e. he has to make the case.

When a firearm is required solely for the purposes of target shooting, the applicant must be a member of a Home Office-approved club. When a firearm is going to be used for hunting, the applicant can demonstrate good reason by having permission to shoot on a suitable piece of land which has the chosen quarry species on it. (In practice, there are few pieces of land that will not have the more common species of quarry on them. Animals have legs and they move about.) Where non-native exotic quarry (e.g. feral goats or wild boar) are applied for, the applicant will have to be very specific that he has permission to shoot these beasts on land where they are known to exist.

If you apply for firearms for the purposes of collecting, you will need to demonstrate that you are a bona fide collector. There are no set criteria for doing this but an academic interest in firearm

development and technology, an established library or membership of a learned society all indicate you are a collector. It is important to note, however, that you do not have to be a member of, say, the Arms and Armour Society or the Historical Breechloading Smallarms Association to be classed as a collector. It is also important that people have individual tastes and interests and guns which might be regarded with disdain by one collector may be the apple of another collector's eye. Collections all have to start somewhere and it is the applicant's genuine intent that counts.

Whereas applicants for firearm certificates must prove their good reason, the same does not hold good for shotgun certificates (SGC). It is assumed that by making the application, you have a 'good reason' for possessing shotguns and the Chief Constable can only refuse to grant the certificate if he has reason to believe that you don't. Consequently, you do not have to be a member of a clay pigeon club or a pheasant shooting syndicate, for example. It is enough to say to the Firearms Enquiry Officer who interviews you that you want to possess the shotgun for broad purposes such as pigeon shooting, wildfowling or game shooting.

Once you have been granted a SGC, it allows you to acquire as many shotguns as you like – providing you have adequate security measures to look after them. A FAC authorises you to acquire specific firearms and if you want to change them or acquire others, you must apply to the police for a variation. Thus to describe matters in terms of the EU Weapons Directive, the guns on a firearm certificate are called 'firearms subject to prior authorisation' i.e. the police must authorise you to possess a specific type of firearm and those on a shotgun certificate are 'firearms subject to notification', i.e. you must tell the police when you acquire or get rid of one.

Dealing with the police

Most people in firearms licensing are not actual police officers but police staff. In the main, they are decent, hard-working people but occasionally (as in all walks of life) you will encounter rude or unhelpful individuals. It is always as well to remember that police staff are public servants and that you are paying for them through your taxes. Accordingly, you are entitled to a reasonable level of service. By the same juncture, being unpleasant to a member of police staff is simply not acceptable and will do nothing to help get you a certificate. Here are some tips to enable you to get the best out of the police:

- Always keep a note of any contact that you have with the licensing department. (Include time, contact name, detail of discussion, promised outcomes and things you have been asked to do.)
- Always keep copies of emails and letters.
- Ask the name of the person to whom you are speaking and refer to them by name during the conversation.
- Always complain to both the Firearms Licensing Manager and the Police and Crime Commissioner if you receive bad service. Conversely, always make a point of praising good service.
- Be courteous but firm.
- Make a timeline of any contact with the police.
- Record any interview with firearms licensing staff. You must say you are doing this. A recording actually protects both parties and, in an age where mobile phones and other IT can do this easily, it makes sense to have an audio-visual record.

Firearms Licensing: Statutory Guidance for Chief Officers of Police

This is perhaps the most important development in firearms licensing in the last twenty years.

The 2015 inspection of police firearms licensing by Her Majesty's Inspectorate of Constabulary and Fire and Rescue Services identified the need for greater consistency in the application of firearms licensing law by Firearms Licensing Departments (FLDs). It recommended that the existing *Home Office Guide on Firearms Licensing Law* be made statutory.

The consultation for this took some eighteen months and the government were just about to issue it when the single incident mass killing (SIMK) took place at Keyham on 12 August 2021. This delayed the matter again and it was not until November 2021 that it was finally issued. Consequently, it is important to note that the statutory guidance was not formulated as a result of the Keyham SIMK; it was merely coincidental to its commencement.

The term 'statutory guidance' is something of a misnomer. Contrary to what the title suggests, chief officers are not compelled to obey its content. However, they must 'have regard to' its provisions. This means that they must have considered them and if they decide to depart from them, they must give their reasons. 'Have regard to' has been defined by the courts in the case of R (on the application of London Oratory School Governors) v The Schools Adjudicator [2015]. Mr Justice Cobb said:

> 'The phrase "have regard to" means to take into account. It does not connotate slavish obedience or deference on every occasion.'

The statutory guidance is principally concerned with a certificate applicant's suitability and its assessment. The biggest impact that its introduction had on the licensing process was the universal requirement for independent medical verification of all applicants (Paragraphs 2.24 – 2.45). There is a great deal of misunderstanding about this with many people thinking that their GP is giving some sort of certificate which says they are suitable to be allowed access to a firearm. This is not so; the Chief Officer makes the final decision about who is granted a certificate.

Medical verification is no more than an initial screen to verify that an applicant's answer to the question at box 9 on the application form corresponds to the content of his medical records. The process of involving medical professionals in firearms licensing has its origin in the case of Christopher Foster in Oswestry in 2008. Foster's business was failing and rather than see his family cut back on an opulent lifestyle, he shot dead his wife and daughter, and slaughtered the family pets before torching his home and committing suicide. He had already expressed suicidal thoughts to his doctor who had not flagged them up to the police. HM Coroner said there needed to be better communication between doctors and patients with access to guns.

The application form (201) asks applicants to declare if they have or have ever been treated for nine medical conditions that are relevant to firearms licensing.

(i) Acute Stress Reaction or an acute reaction to the stress caused by a trauma, including post-traumatic stress disorder;
(ii) suicidal thoughts or self-harm or harm to others;
(iii) depression or anxiety;
(iv) dementia;
(v) mania, bipolar disorder, or a psychotic illness;
(vi) a personality disorder;
(vii) a neurological condition: for example, Multiple Sclerosis, Parkinson's or Huntington's diseases, or epilepsy;
(viii) alcohol or drug abuse; and
(ix) any other mental or physical condition, or combination of conditions, which may affect the safe possession of firearms or shotguns.

The first eight are all conditions which common sense confirms could have a bearing on the safe possession of firearms. Number nine is a catch-all; if you think you may suffer from any such condition, ask your doctor. Bear in mind that anyone who knowingly or recklessly makes a false statement in order to be granted a certificate commits an offence by doing so. On that basis it is always better to play safe and declare something, rather than conceal it only to have it become a contentious issue later.

There is no intention by the government to introduce some form of psychometric testing for anyone who wants to own firearms. It is recognised that this would bring no benefit to the licensing process. The idea was dismissed as recently as November 1996 by the Parliamentary Office of Science and Technology. It said that 'Most experts conclude, therefore that the clinical approach to assessing dangerousness is a non-starter for screening gun applicants'.

There is still a huge social stigma about mental illness; there is no shame in admitting you suffer from it. Admitting you are unwell is halfway to being cured. In any case, it is not an absolute barrier to being granted a certificate. I know of several people who suffer from depression but manage their conditions successfully. Their licensing departments recognise this and accept that they benefit from the feelings of wellbeing that their shooting brings them. The main thing is to get your doctor on your side when you apply. An application that admits to problems, but which has a doctor's support is hard to refuse.

Sometimes an applicant's GP will not participate in this process, often for what is laughably referred to as 'conscientious objection'. That does not matter, as there are alternatives available. BASC members can use the BASC medical panel, a service which is an exclusive membership benefit. There are other commercial providers who can be located online. The test of validity of a doctor to provide registration is that he/she has to be registered with the General Medical Council. It should be remembered that an applicant's GP cannot charge for supplying a patient a copy of his medical records and has to do that within twenty-eight days or two months for complex cases.

Paragraph 2.25 makes it plain that medical verification needs to be provided at both grant and renewal. Paragraph 2.15 also clarifies that a home visit is required of an applicant on the initial grant of a certificate. However, it also allows for the possibility of renewal being conducted by telephone, video call or email rather than the expensive and, in the majority of cases, wholly needless home visit. (Anecdotal evidence given to BASC by a senior police officer involved in licensing was that only 2 per cent of applicants give cause for concern on renewal.)

Paragraphs 2.55 and 2.56 deals with the circumstances that should be considered when deciding whether a visit or a risk-assessed renewal would be appropriate.

(i) Certificate held for at least two cycles (ten years);
(ii) not having come to police attention adversely in the previous two cycles for matters other than minor road-traffic infringements;
(iii) no concerns regarding firearms matters, such as discrepancies in serial numbers;
(iv) no calls of an adverse nature to address in previous five years;
(v) no intelligence suggesting criminality on behalf of certificate holder or associates;
(vi) recent contact with GP and no concerns raised;
(vii) no concerns raised by referees.

Any applicant who ticks all these boxes should not need a home visit to renew his/her certificate. Paradoxically, one of the beneficial aspects of the Covid pandemic saw the police having to rely on IT-based methods to conduct renewals; there is no reason why this should not continue. Home visits are the most expensive of all licensing processes as they take a lot of time. Anything that reduces their frequency has universal benefits for police efficiency. This, in turn, keeps certificate fees down.

Paragraph 2.45 lists the additional enquiries that a chief officer may make in order to provide additional information about an applicant's general suitability.

   (i) Checks with other agencies, such as health professionals other than the GP, social services, probation services or multi-agency groups;
  (ii) checks with other licensing or regulatory bodies or Government enforcement agencies;
 (iii) a drug or alcohol test;
 (iv) credit or other financial checks;
  (v) information obtained from open-source social media.

The last two merit some explanation. Someone who is in debt might be vulnerable to blackmail, especially if the debt has been incurred by way of criminality (e.g. drugs). Social-media feeds are unlikely to be subject to routine scrutiny and will probably be focused on someone who has already come to the notice of the police. In my opinion, having a social-media account automatically prejudices the holding of a certificate; I have seen too many people lose their certificates as a result of ill-advised, off-the-cuff comments on social media. My advice is to steer well clear of it, although such advice may not be palatable in these days of almost universal social-media addiction. (See my further remarks on this later on.)

A large section of the guidance deals with domestic violence (DV). That is very much flavour-of-the-month with Government and the merest hint that a certificate holder is associated with DV is likely to prove fatal for certificate holding. Certificate holders are very vulnerable to malicious comments made by disgruntled spouses and partners eager to extract revenge when a relationship breaks up. If you think that the breakdown of a relationship is likely to end acrimoniously, then store your guns elsewhere than at home (e.g. with a friend or registered firearms dealer). That way you cannot be accused of threatening a spouse or partner with them as they would not be in your immediate possession.

Part 3 of the statutory guidance deals with factors which might indicate someone is unsuitable to hold a certificate. Obviously previous criminal behaviour will almost certainly stop someone being granted/renewing a certificate for a long time to come. Even in the case of an acquittal in court, the chief officer is still entitled to test the matter on a lower burden of proof than would be required for the criminal standard for a conviction. The police apply the old principle of 'No smoke without fire', regardless.

Paragraph 3.9 lists information that may indicate unsuitability to hold a certificate:

(i) associations with known criminals or suspected criminals, including members of gangs or organised crime groups, or associations with terrorist or proscribed groups or organisations; or aggressive, abusive, or anti-social behaviour or incitement to hatred against particular groups categorised by for example, race, gender, disability, sexual orientation, age, or religion;
(ii) evidence of dishonesty;
(iii) evidence of threatening or abusive behaviour;

- (iv) evidence of anti-social behaviour;
- (v) evidence of reckless behaviour, lack of self-control or restraint, or disregard for the safety of others;
- (vi) indications that the individual will not handle the firearm responsibly
- (vii) insufficiently secure storage arrangements;
- (viii) relationship difficulties or other domestic turmoil;
- (ix) unmanaged debts, financial pressures, abnormal financial activity, or unexplained sources of income;
- (x) relevant medical conditions including alcohol and drug abuse
- (xi) previous non-compliance with firearms certificate or other types of licences held; and
- (xii) any of the above factors in relation to a person other than the certificate holder living at, or with unsupervised access to, the address or addresses.

The converse also applies; in addition to the factors above, chief officers should consider any positive evidence supporting the application, for example, evidence of rehabilitation, change in circumstances, good character, or a history of responsible ownership of firearms.

Chief officers are required to have processes in place to continually assess a certificate holder. Whilst this may seem intrusive and smack of Big Brother, it's actually beneficial to the shooting community in the long term. If the private ownership of firearms is to continue in the UK, then the public has to have confidence in the licensing system. Also, medical verification and continuous assessment are the foundations for getting certificate life increased. With them successfully established, there is no reason why a certificate should not be valid for ten years or longer.

Unannounced visits

The guidance says that these should only be made when credible, particular intelligence is received in light of a particular threat or risk of harm. In deciding whether to make an unannounced visit, the police have to judge this action on public safety grounds which have to be deemed to be proportionate and justified. The police are not expected to undertake visits at anti-social times unless there is a real need for them to do so. They should be prepared to give evidence of this. The police should also be able to give a proper explanation as why they are calling without a prior appointment. Vague statements like 'We were in the area' or 'it's just routine' will not be acceptable. The best way of dealing with any police staff member who turns up unannounced and without a search warrant is to control entry by means of a door chain and spyhole. With those security measures in place, you control who gets in or out. Video footage taken on a mobile phone is very useful as are photographs of faces, ID etc. People are much more likely to behave properly if they know they can be easily identified.

Firearms licensing personnel have no statutory right of entry into your home. However, someone who gives a valid reason for a visit and is co-operative should not be obstructed needlessly. The last sentence in Paragraph 4.8 puts it well:

> 'To mitigate any misunderstanding on the part of the certificate holder, the police should provide a clear and reasoned explanation to the certificate holder at the time of the visit.'

Co-operation is a two-way street which does not admit of excess by either party. For example, a firearms enquiry officer who turns up at eleven o'clock at night and demands entry without a reason should not be admitted and should be complained about to Professional Standards. Equally, a self-entitled, barrack-room lawyer certificate holder who turns down a polite and detailed explanation from a member of police staff as to why he seeks admission will probably find himself under suitability review. Rudeness from either party puts them in the wrong straight away.

Suitability reviews

Sometimes a licensing department will receive information about a certificate holder that creates sufficient concern about that person's suitability to possess firearms, but does not justify immediate revocation but still requires further investigation. In order to give the certificate holder, the benefit of any doubt, but to eradicate any risk by his continuing possession of them he will be asked to voluntarily surrender 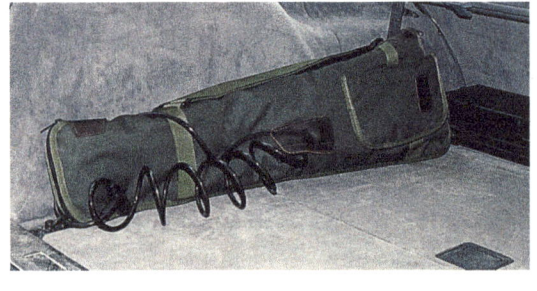 them and his certificate(s) pending further investigation. There is no formal mechanism in law to do this and the choice will always remain that of the certificate holder. Such a request for so-called 'voluntary surrender' should always be backed by reasons and if these are not given then strong consideration should be given to decline the request. As stated earlier, co-operation is a two-way street and both parties have to act reasonably and proportionately.

One issue that constantly crops up concerning suitability reviews is that no receipt for the guns is provided. The other is the inordinate length of time taken to make a decision to resolve the matter. (BASC is aware of cases taking years to be decided.) All too often, once someone's guns are in police custody there is no incentive to progress matters. This is wholly unacceptable. The statutory guidance recognises this and makes the following remarks at 4.10 & 4.11.

'When firearms are surrendered or seized, ammunition and the certificate should also be seized, and a receipt and photograph provided detailing the firearms, accessories and ammunition removed. Following surrender or seizure of firearms, a full review should be carried out and the certificate holder advised of the result of the review. The certificate holder should be kept informed of the progress of the review at frequent and regular intervals. Should the review conclude that there is no danger to public safety or the peace, the firearms, ammunition and certificates should be returned, subject to the relevant authorisation.'

In light of this, there can now be no excuse for receipts not to be issued and the condition of the gun(s) documented by photographs. Any officer who refuses to do this should be the subject of a formal complaint to Professional Standards. The same applies to any licensing decision maker who fails to progress the review and who fails to keep the certificate holder informed about such progress. The ultimate sanction available against police staff who fail to abide by the terms of the statutory guidance is to complain to the Police and Crime Commissioner that the chief officer is failing to 'have regard to' the guidance by failing to supervise his staff. That is likely to concentrate minds.

The rest of the statutory guidance concerns administrative matters for the police. Every certificate holder should read and understand the statutory guidance as it sets out how the police should operate and behave. It is available online at:

https://assets.publishing.service.gov.uk/government/uploads/system/uploads/attachment_data/file/1029859/Statutory_Guidance_for_Firearms_Licensing_-_Final__Nov_2021_.pdf

Residency qualifications

In order to be granted a certificate you must be resident in Great Britain. You do not have to be a GB national.

There is case law on whether you are a resident or not. The leading case is Burditt v Joslin [1981]. In this case, Colonel Burditt had been posted to the British Army of the Rhine (BAOR) and had let his GB residence. The court found he was not a resident as he did not have unfettered access to his property. By the same token, a student living in digs during term time who still comes home to his parents' house in the

holidays is a GB resident. Likewise, someone who works abroad on a short-term contract and returns to his home while on leave is too.

The case of Mills-Owen v Chief Constable of Hampshire [2003] establishes that a person can have more than one residence but residence at one particular home will be a matter of evidence.

The four conditions

These appear on every FAC and SGC by law and it is a criminal offence (potentially punishable by a large fine and/or imprisonment) not to abide by them.

1) The holder must, on receipt of the certificate, sign it in ink with his usual signature.

This is self-explanatory but it is amazing how many people don't do this. I have known somebody fined for not signing the certificate, although in this case there were other charges that could not be proved and it seemed the police wanted to ensure he paid a fine for something.

2) The holder of the certificate must, inform the chief officer of police by whom it was granted as soon as reasonably practicable, but within seven days of the theft, loss or destruction in Great Britain of the certificate and/or the theft or loss, deactivation or destruction of any shotguns to which this certificate relates.

Again, this is self-explanatory. If a certificate gets badly damaged or worn out, the police have to replace it, providing you can produce the remnants. If you lose the certificate altogether, you have to pay for a new one.

3) The holder of this certificate must, without undue delay, inform the chief officer of police by whom the certificate was granted of any change of permanent address.

This condition needs a little clarification. There is no legal definition of 'permanent address' as it is really a matter of fact and degree in each case. Some indicators of permanence might be: the address where you are registered to vote, where you pay council tax and where utility bills or bank correspondence are sent. However, the term-time address of a student is clearly not permanent, even if the course is of several years' duration and he/she spends more time there than he/she does at home. Equally, the digs of a person working  away from home for several months is not a permanent address either.

'Without undue delay' means what it says and there is no fixed time period. It would be reasonable for someone to take a fortnight to settle into his new home, unpack his household goods and fix his cabinet to the wall before telling the police he had moved. However, it would not be reasonable to take six months to do it. That would constitute undue delay. It is important to recognise the difference in the language between conditions two and three.

When you decide to notify the police that you have moved all you have to do is tell the chief officer of the force that issued your certificate your new address and leave him or her to do the rest. Do not do that until you have installed your cabinet or other security measures. Do not send in your old certificate either; you need it to prove legal ownership of firearms/shotguns and to buy ammunition. It remains valid in Great Britain even though you may have moved. You can exchange it for the new one when it is ready.

When you move you do not have to complete the application forms again. It is likely that a firearm enquiry officer will come round to make sure that your security is acceptable. Photos of the cabinet(s) in its new location(s) can be sent by email and a laptop/phone camera can be used to provide live feed. Beyond that you don't have to do anything.

It is very important that you do tell the police when you move. Colleagues from firearms licensing tell me that a huge amount of time is spent trying to track down certificate holders who have moved without telling them. Knowing where certificate holders live is a fundamental tenet of the licensing system. It is as well to send notification of a move by recorded delivery and check the tracking number for the signature of receipt. Take a copy of the letter too. If you use permitted electronic means (i.e. to the firearms licensing email address on the police website), ask for a read receipt and keep a paper copy. In the event of any argument about whether you notified or not, the police would have to prove (beyond reasonable doubt) that you didn't. Proof that you had told them would put you in an unassailable position.

4) Condition 4 is the most important on the certificate and also the most complicated. It is split into two parts and covers the security of your firearms. It is vitally important that you abide by its terms because a gun that is lost or stolen because of personal slackness is an own goal for shooting that could be exploited by anti-gun groups. It will certainly attract the revocation of your certificate and you will lose your shooting for the foreseeable future; you may even be prosecuted and face a large fine or even imprisonment on conviction. Guns are generally valuable items and you don't want to lose one any more than you would your car. However, the consequences are much more serious and it would be hard to live with the knowledge that someone had been killed or injured by a gun that you had lost by carelessness.

Part (a) of condition 4 on a FAC says that: 'The firearms and ammunition to which this certificate relates must at all times (except in the circumstances set out in paragraph (b) below) be stored securely to prevent, so far as is reasonably practicable, access to the firearms and ammunition by an unauthorised person.' The SGC has similar wording but does not refer to shotgun ammunition.

This part of the condition refers to the times when you are not using your gun(s). The operative words are 'reasonably practicable' which are defined in law. They come from a Court of Appeal case of Edwards v National Coal Board [1949] and mean that you have to take measures (called sacrifices) that are not grossly disproportionate to the risk itself. For instance it would be grossly disproportionate to install a security system costing £20,000 to protect a single shotgun. However, it would not be disproportionate to spend £100 on a cabinet to achieve the same aim.

'Reasonable' is also defined in law, after the leading case of Associated Provincial Picture Houses v Wednesbury Corporation [1947]. 'Reasonableness' is a personal thing that relates to an individual's own situation at a specific time and is not a blanket concept applicable to everybody all the time. It implies that a middle course must be steered between two extremes. In security terms, these extremes range between very expensive security systems, for example a biometrically controlled vault, and the completely lackadaisical practice of leaving a shotgun propped up behind the kitchen door.

For most people the easiest solution to obeying this statutory condition is to lock their guns in a steel cabinet. There is nothing in law that says it must conform to the British Standard, BS 7558 of 1992. (This was only based on the resistance to attack by a person with hammer, chisel and wrecking bar for two five-minute periods. While most cabinets sold in the UK will be to the British Standard, there are others which are not and are equally as good.)

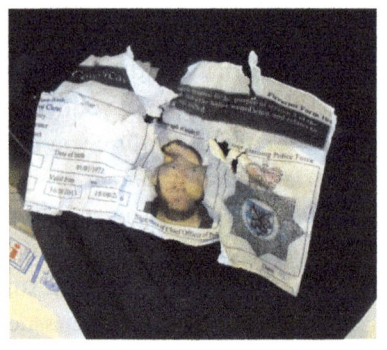

Here are some basic security ideas that might help you.

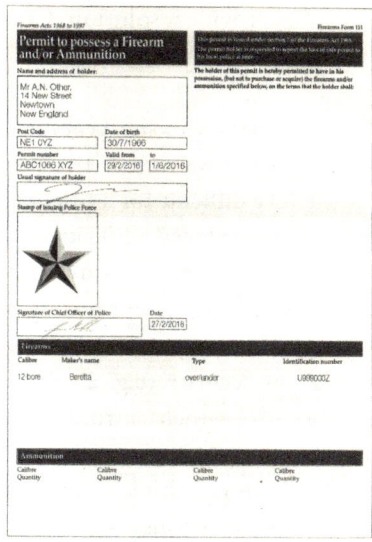

- If you choose to use a cabinet, site it somewhere that is convenient to you. If it is not easy to access, basic human nature says that you will not use it. A cabinet in a hard-to-get-at place may be very secure but it can't protect your gun if you don't put your gun in it because you are too tired after a hard day's rough shooting.

- Try to hide the cabinet.
  If a burglar does not know it is there he can't attack it. I think camouflage is the most important principle of security. Site the cabinet out of view of visitors to your home. Don't excite natural curiosity.

- Most manufacturers give their products a nominal capacity, e.g. four-gun cabinet. Contrary to what some sections of the police may believe, this does not mean that it is not suitable to hold more than four guns. This is merely a descriptor for marketing purposes. Its true capacity is however many guns you can get in it and still lock the door.

- Always anchor the cabinet to the fabric of the building. Otherwise, it just becomes a convenient case in which to carry away your guns. Remember that expander bolts only work in brick or stone walls. There are also self-tapping masonry screws that are very effective. In these days of stud or plasterboard walls, modern glues may provide a solution. Coach bolts screwed into floor joists are an effective anchor.

- A good way to site a cabinet, for example, is to lay it on its back in a built in wardrobe. This probably doubles its capacity and makes it very difficult for a thief to attack as your upper body strength is greatly reduced while kneeling. If you cover it with carpet and put some shoes on it, then it will look for all the world like a length of central heating pipe boxing.

- Point security (e.g. a cabinet), is only as good as the perimeter security which surrounds it. Passive infrared lights deter casual burglars. It is also common sense to fit good door and window locks. If you think of it as layers surrounding your cabinet, you will not go far wrong.

- There is no point at which the number of guns you own triggers the need to install an alarm. See Chapter 18 of the Home Office Guide for suggestions of when it thinks that alarms might be merited. The principle of 'each case on its merits' holds good.

Always base your security measures on what is known as 'target hardening'. It is a very useful concept based on the Four Ds.

DENY – a thief easy access to your home.
DETER – a thief by physical security measures.
DISGUISE – don't invite a thief by displaying attractive objects to him.
DEFLECT – a thief away from your home towards an easier target.

One of the first cases that I ever handled for BASC was in Newcastle Crown Court in January 1991. It concerned security and whether the

appellant's gun cabinet was up to the job. The chief officer said it was not because it did not conform to a blanket policy that he had. The would-be certificate holder said that it was an effective deterrent. The learned judge, His Honour Judge Stephenson summed up security as 'a series of difficulties' presented to a burglar. His words stuck in my mind and I have never forgotten them. I think they are the soundest practical advice you can get.

Chapter 18 of the Home Office Guide deals with security and is essential reading. It stresses (at 18.16): 'The Rules do not prescribe the form of safekeeping or security. As with most aspects of crime prevention, the police must look at the individual circumstances of each case and at the overall security arrangements that will be in place. The level of security should be proportionate to the risk and each case must be judged on its merits. A firearm is like any other property which needs protecting from the burglar/housebreaker or thief. Advice should be balanced and reasonable as well as comprehensive'. There are many ways of securing guns and personal situations must be catered for.

The police are not allowed to have blanket policies when exercising a statutory function. Any policy must not be punitive and must always admit exceptions if it is to be lawful. The leading case is R v Wakefield Crown Court, ex parte Oldfield [1977].

If you want to go deeper into security, for example making your own gunroom, then the Home Office *Firearms Security Handbook 2020* is for you. It is a joint effort between the shooting associations, the police and the Home Office. While it can be a bit clumsy to use and wordy in parts, it is nonetheless sound. It is available online at: www.gov.uk/government/publications.

The second part of the condition (4 b) covers those situations when the gun is either in use or you are doing something to it. Condition 4 b) says that: 'Where a firearm and/or ammunition (or a shotgun but not shotgun ammunition) to which this certificate related is in use or the holder of the certificate has it with him/her for the purposes of cleaning, repairing or testing it or for some other purpose connected with its use, transfer or sale, or the firearm (shotgun) or ammunition is in transit to or from a place in connection with its use or any such purpose, reasonable precautions must be taken for the safe custody of the firearm and/or ammunition.'

In this case the operative words are 'reasonable precautions must be taken for the safe custody'. We already know what 'reasonable' means. 'Safe custody' means safe keeping or protection. It is as well to be aware that the condition says 'has with him/her' so the overarching meaning of this condition is that the certificate holder will look after the gun while he is doing something with it. The opposite is that when he is not doing something with it, then the gun need not be with him, but it must be secured away.

Condition 4 (b) imposes a lesser standard of responsibility but it must still be looked at in terms of what a reasonable person would do in those particular circumstances.

Other conditions

The law allows the Chief Constable to impose other conditions on a firearm certificate only (see Sections 10.10 – 10.15 of the Guide). It is a criminal offence to fail to comply with these conditions. Section 10.11 makes the very good point that 'they should only be used, where the individual circumstances require it for public safety'. The next section says that every effort must be made to limit the number of additional conditions imposed on a firearm certificate and to ensure that they are not contradictory'. (See Appendix 3 for the wording of the Home Office recommended conditions.) In my view, any condition that is so badly written as to be contradictory can be safely ignored.

When you are initially granted a certificate it will be limited to 'land deemed suitable' by the chief officer. This means that you must ascertain that the land has been checked as being suitable for the type of rifle and cartridge. Most police forces will have a sort of land registry and a simple phone call will suffice. The landowner may know as well. After a time (not specified) you can apply for the deemed suitable words to be removed. In that case you make your own decision about whether the land is safe to shoot over. Competence is normally demonstrated by the use of ammunition as recorded on the certificate. Most applications for the less-restrictive condition will not be entertained during the first year of certificate life, but each case must be taken on its merits.

The condition will also refer to 'any lawful' quarry – aka the AOLQ condition. This means just what it says; if it is legal to shoot it, you may. Many forward-thinking police forces apply the AOLQ on the grant of a firearm certificate; they should be applauded for their common-sense approach.

There is a right of appeal against a decision to refuse to vary an existing condition, but none against the initial decision to impose one.

Where shotgun certificates are concerned, they may be specially conditioned to refer to shotguns disguised as other objects to allow the acquisition of walking stick or umbrella guns. Other than the statutory conditions, this is the only additional condition that may be imposed on a shotgun certificate.

Travelling with guns

Here are a few tips as to how you might satisfy that statutory security requirement when you are using or travelling with your gun.

- When firearms or ammunition are transported in a vehicle they must be concealed from view. The rear passenger footwell is a good choice, covered by coats or travel rugs.

- If you need to stop, try to park your vehicle in a well-lit area, within the range of any CCTV cameras and where you can see it.

- Remove some vital part from the gun and take it with you. If you have taken the bolt out of a rifle, it becomes nothing more than a club. Taking the forend off a shotgun will not normally stop it from being fired. However, it will take a while for the thief to learn how to re-cock the mechanism and will also show that you were thinking about firearm security when you took it away.

- You should always do your best not to leave a complete firearm and ammunition in an unattended vehicle.

- Always lock the vehicle and set the alarm if one is fitted.

- It is always a good idea to park a car in a spot with restricted access e.g. with the tailgate so close to a wall that it cannot be opened.

- A cable lock through a trigger guard enhances security and some companies offer purpose-made slips or covers which incorporate a locked cable. If you were to use one of these, it would be very hard to prosecute you if you had a gun stolen.

- Security is a matter of being 'aware' and of using your common sense by avoiding potentially risky situations. In these times of increased terrorist activity, it is vitally important to be extra vigilant about the security of your personal firearm(s).

Guns in overnight accommodation

If your sport takes you away from home, you will need to know what to do to secure your gun(s) while in temporary accommodation. As a general rule it is never wise to let hotel staff know that you have a gun with you. Most people are not familiar with guns and tend to panic when they encounter them. This invariably leads to the police being called and a lot of grief usually ensues because your average bobby does not know about sporting guns either. I have heard of people spending several hours in police stations

for questioning while matters were being sorted out. Some people even lost an expensive day's shooting because the police hung onto their guns. This is particularly the case in large chain hotels in urban areas. Their staff will have no idea about sporting guns and in this risk-averse climate, they will call the police just to cover themselves.

It goes without saying that you should never ask hotel staff to store your gun(s) as it would be illegal for them to do so. I have heard of some hotels that are used to shooters staying, having gun cabinets on offer. That is all well and good but if hotel staff retain a duplicate set of keys, then they have access to your guns and an offence is committed by all parties.

It is always a good idea to bring your gun into the hotel in a non-gun shaped case to avoid drawing attention to it. Most broken down shotguns can easily be accommodated in a conventional suitcase. Some hand luggage is made with a special compartment for barrels that is concealed within the bag. Long, rigid gun cases like those made for rifles can be made to look less obvious by the addition of labels which imply they have inoffensive contents. I used to kid people I was carrying a trombone by having a Musicians' Union sticker on my rifle case! Use your imagination. What people don't know about, they won't worry about.

If you intend to stay in a guest house or B&B, a phone call ascertaining that the owner is comfortable with you bringing guns into their home never hurts. If they don't like the idea, vote with your feet and stay elsewhere.

Consider dividing your shotgun between your hotel room and car with the barrels in one and the stock and action in the other. That way it would be very unlikely for a complete gun to be stolen.

Remove vital components (rifle bolts, forends, etc.) and carry them about with you. There are special bolt holsters that slip on a belt; shopping bags are handy for carrying/concealing larger forends. Using them stops a complete firearm being taken. Some hotel rooms offer guests small combination safes which are very handy for storing rifle ammunition and small components.

Cable locks secured to central heating pipes or similar fixtures offer useful portable security but bear in mind that most trigger guards are inherently weak and can be unscrewed.

One especially creative solution to security would be to use a cable lock to secure the gun to the bath rails, conceal it with the shower curtain and lock the bathroom door with a coin from the outside. Switch the wireless on and hang the 'Do Not Disturb' sign on the handle. That way any thief will never be sure that the room is empty and will be deflected to try elsewhere.

Shooting near buildings, roads, etc.

There is no offence of shooting near a building although it is not good manners if the occupants are inconvenienced or distressed by you doing so. It is also possible that if you shoot near farm buildings housing valuable livestock that injures itself as a result of panicking at the noise, then you might end up being sued for damages. It is also possible to be prosecuted for criminal damage, for example, you knew that a brood mare might abort her foal if alarmed by your gunshots, but went on and shot anyway. A court might find you were reckless by doing so and convict.

We all have a duty to be considerate and courteous to other countryside users, so think about where you are going to shoot. Equally, we should not stop our reasonable activities just because someone does not approve of shooting. Try to achieve a balance. Good neighbourliness costs nothing and always brings its own rewards.

Equally there is no offence of shooting near a footpath. If you have permission to shoot on land either side then you may shoot over it, if safe to do so. Watch out for dog walkers and riders, though. Bear in mind that the purpose of a footpath is to allow people to pass and re-pass (Harrison v Duke of Rutland [1893]), so shooting while standing on one is not a good idea.

When it comes to shooting near roads, there is one piece of legislation of which we should all be aware. Section 161 of the Highways Act 1980 makes it an offence to shoot within 50 feet (15 m) of the centre of the highway if, as a consequence of which a user of the highway is injured, endangered or interrupted. The offence is a conditional one and is committed not just by shooting within 50 feet; it has to be accompanied by one or more of the following three things as well:

Injure; this is a matter of fact. Was someone hurt by you?

Endanger; this is a matter of opinion. A test might be were there realistic prospects that someone might have been hurt?

Interrupt; again a matter of opinion. Did the passer-by have to stop because it was unsafe to proceed?

It is also an offence under Section 28 of the Town Police Clauses Act 1847 'to wantonly discharge any firearm in a street to the obstruction, danger or annoyance of residents or passengers'.

In Scotland, it is also an offence under the common law to discharge a firearm anywhere in a reckless or culpable manner – no injury needs to be caused. The test would be that the shooter showed a gratuitous disregard for the safety of other people. The term 'reckless' has to be construed according to its ordinary meaning, i.e. were you heedless of danger or the consequences of your actions.

Face away from a road, building or footpath while shooting and if in doubt, don't shoot at all.

Falling shot

Many people are alarmed by shotgun pellets falling on them. Mostly, you would never notice, but shot which falls on dead leaves or corrugated iron roofs makes a pattering sound. A birdshot pellet (any under BB size) that falls under the force of gravity is totally harmless and has minimal kinetic energy (KE). For instance, a No6 shot coming from the muzzle of a shotgun under the propulsion of combustion gases at 1,070 fps has 2.8 ft lb of energy at 20 yards; falling under the influence of gravity it has a miniscule kinetic energy value of 0.0247 ft lb. (This is less than the KE of a large hailstone).

It is always as well to bear this in mind as there are often claims that cars and solar panels have been damaged by falling shot. I once shot at a scrap car door at 100 yards (it was difficult to hit) and at that range, the pellets left small black marks that rubbed off with a handkerchief. The metal was not dented and the paint was not chipped.

Be aware when siting gun pegs or clay traps that No6 shot will travel about 220 yards in still conditions and 348 yards with a Force 8 wind behind it. At the risk of repeating myself, it is not very neighbourly to shower someone else in shot on a regular basis.

Allowing shotgun pellets to fall on some else's premises or land is not a criminal offence and is a constructive trespass at best. Nonetheless, in the interests of good relations with others it is best avoided. While falling shotgun pellets are a potential irritant, a rifle bullet at the end of its trajectory is still dangerous. Bullets are pointed, relatively heavy and travel at very high velocities for very long distances. A 172 grain .30 calibre bullet starting with a muzzle velocity of 2,600 fps will travel some 5,500 yards – that is just over 3 miles. As a general rule, when shooting with a shotgun shoot at the sky; with a rifle, make sure there is a safe backstop (e.g. earth) behind your target in case you miss or the bullet passes through it.

Anyone who shoots an airgun pellet (deliberately or accidentally) over the boundary of the land where he has permission to shoot commits a criminal offence (Section 34, Violent Crime Reduction Act 2006). In the case of a young person under 14, whose use of an air rifle must be supervised by a person aged 21 or over at all times, both youngster and supervising adult commit offences under the Anti-Social Behaviour Act 2003. It always pays to watch where you are shooting.

Replacement certificates

There will be times when you need to ask the police for a replacement certificate. This will include:
- When it has become damaged or illegible.
- When you have lost it.
- When there is no space for further entries.

Section 32 of the 1968 Act provides that a fee is payable if the certificate is lost or destroyed. The Guide (10.32 and 11.17) recommends that a 'certificate should be replaced without fee if it is very dirty, mutilated, or lacks space for further legible entries to be made'.

If the police agree to replace it quickly then give them the old certificate. If they indicate it will take some time, then hold on to the old certificate; you will need it to prove lawful possession of firearms or to buy ammunition. Give it to the police when your new one arrives.

Temporary permits

Section 7 of the Firearms Act 1968 allows a chief officer to issue a temporary permit to allow someone to hold firearms, their ammunition or shotguns without holding the relevant certificate. The issue of a temporary permit is entirely discretionary and there is no right of appeal against a refusal. There are no stated circumstances when a temporary permit

can be issued and each case has to be judged on its merits. Perhaps the most common reason for their issue is to help the heirs of a dead certificate holder by giving them authority to hold his or her firearms and ammunition on a temporary basis until a decision has been made about their disposal.

Anyone who has applied for the renewal of his certificate in good time and is due to expire shortly, should apply for a temporary permit under Section 7 of the Firearms Act 1968. It is an absolute offence to possess firearms and ammunition without a certificate. If you are ever told otherwise by a police representative, you should disregard any such assurances. The police do not have the power to switch the law on and off. A certificate that has expired is not valid in any circumstances. This is confirmed by Paragraph 6.6 of the Home Office Statutory Guidance:

> 'Certificate holders must not be asked to rely on an expired certificate or registration. It is unlawful for them to do so.'

The police do not like issuing temporary permits because they allege that it causes them as much work as issuing a renewed certificate. (That statement is doubtful; I am reliably informed by a former licensing manager that a Section 7 can be produced at the press of a button.) Be resolute in the face of a refusal to grant one and make a note of the full name and other details of the person who refuses. Any such refusal should be challenged by writing to the Police and Crime Commissioner. Do not be concerned that making a complaint will be regarded as a black mark against you thereafter. In my experience the opposite normally happens: you will be treated with kid gloves.

While a temporary permit authorises possession of Section 1 & 2 firearms and ammunition, it does not extend to prohibited items, for example expanding ammunition or historic handguns held under Section 7(1) of the 1997 Act. If it looks like you are going to be left in illegal possession of such items by the expiry of your certificate then you should ask a dealer with the requisite authority to store them for you. It goes without saying that the reasonable costs of such an exercise should be passed on to the chief officer.

The police can put whatever conditions they please on a temporary permit. However, if issued to cover an expired certificate, any condition which does not allow the use of the firearms to which it refers is manifestly unreasonable and should be challenged.

Section 28(B) of the Firearms Act 1968 provides that there shall be an automatic extension of eight weeks to the life of an expired firearm or shotgun certificate, providing that the application to renew the certificate was made before eight weeks of its expiry date.

BASC does not carry a brief for anyone who has failed to submit their renewal application in reasonable time.

Carrying your certificate

There is no legal requirement for you to carry your certificate while you are out with your guns. However, it is sensible to do so. Section 48 of the 1968 Act allows a constable to demand to see a certificate from anyone he or she believes to be in possession of a firearm, shotgun or ammunition. If you cannot produce a certificate, the officer may 'seize and detain' the firearm, shotgun or ammunition and require your name and address from you (it is an offence to refuse to give it or to give a false one). It is likely to be very inconvenient to have your gun(s) and ammunition seized. It could also prove very expensive if that causes you to lose a day's shooting.

A sensible constable would accept the evidence of a photocopy, but don't forget that if you photocopy most certificates, the security paper upon which they are printed comes out with 'Fake' written on it. This might lead to further complications. I think it is good practice to carry your certificate when using or carrying your gun(s). If you do that, then you are 'bombproof'. After all if the certificate gets damaged, for example soaked when you fall in a ditch, then the police have to replace it free of charge.

Guns in public

It is an offence under Section 19 of the 1968 Act (as amended Section 37(1) by the Anti-social Behaviour Act 2003) to have with you in a public place – unless you can show lawful authority or reasonable excuse – the following:

- A loaded shotgun.
- An air weapon (whether it is loaded or not).
- Any other firearm (whether it is loaded or not) together with ammunition suitable for use in it.
- An imitation firearm.

The 1968 Act defines a 'public place' to include 'any highway and any other premises or place to which at the material time the public have or are permitted to have access, whether on payment or otherwise'. To give examples of this, the showroom area of a shop is a public place, whereas the storeroom and area behind the counter is not. A game fair or country show is a public place but your garden is not. A canal towpath is a public place but farmland is not.

By extension, if you take your shotgun to a game fair to shoot in a clay target competition, you have reasonable excuse; the same would apply if you took a stalking rifle and its ammunition to a gunsmith to have the scope zeroed. Taking your air rifle onto the towpath for some plinking would not constitute a reasonable excuse. However, the shooting tenants on a grouse moor to which the public has access under the Countryside Rights of Way Act 2006, (right-to-roam) still have reasonable excuse to shoot although members of the public are not restrained from being there.

For all that some situations are clearly reasonable or unreasonable; the words 'reasonable excuse' must always be considered within the particular circumstances of the situation. (See my earlier comments about reasonableness.)

The term 'lawful authority' refers to members of the armed services and police officers carrying a service firearm while on duty and does not mean that the person has a firearm or shotgun certificate.

The Firearms Act makes no reference to a gun having to be carried in a slip or a case while in public. However, it is common sense to do so, otherwise you risk being shot by armed officers. My earlier comments about not carrying guns in cases which are gun shaped also apply here.

In law the term 'loaded firearm' has a specific meaning which is not reflected in common speech. It is defined as 'a shotgun or air weapon shall be deemed to be loaded if there is ammunition in the chamber or the barrel or in any magazine or other device which is in such a position the ammunition can be fed into the chamber or barrel by the manual or automatic operation of some part of the gun or weapon'. Essentially this means that a gun is considered loaded if it has 'one up the spout' or cartridges in a magazine attached to the gun.

Shooting without certificates

As a general principle, the UK's firearms law is based on the premise that you need some form of authority to possess firearms. However, the law also recognises that there are times when people should be allowed to possess a gun without a certificate on a temporary basis, providing they conform to certain legal requirements. It is not the case that if you hold a certificate for a particular gun, then you can allow anyone to have a go with it. The exemptions from the need to hold a certificate are very tightly drawn and all the criteria within them must be met otherwise both parties commit an offence.

The majority of exemptions are to be found in Section 11 of the 1968 Act and cover target shooting, race starting, game shooting and shooting clays. These are the ones that relate to country shooting:

Section 11(1) is intended for gun bearers or loaders on formal shoots, for example a loader in a grouse butt or on a driven shoot where double guns are being used. It says that 'a person carrying a firearm or ammunition belonging to another person holding a certificate under this Act may, without himself holding a certificate, have in his possession that firearm or ammunition under instructions from, and for the use of, that other person for sporting purposes only'. It should be noted that this does not allow the bearer to use the gun(s) himself. The courts have found that this exemption does not allow unaccompanied possession. A chauffer was once asked by his employer to carry his guns up to Scotland where he would then meet him off the plane from the continent. The court found that this was not a legitimate use of this exemption and that this was illegal with both employer and chauffer committing offences.

Section 11A – Firearms Act 1968

The Policing and Crime Act 2017 changed the way that non-certificate holders are allowed to borrow firearms. A new Section –

11A was created which combined the exemption at 11(5) of the 1968 Act (shotguns) with Section 16 of the 1988 Amendment Act (rifles).

Section 11(A) allows a non-certificate holder to borrow a shotgun (for live quarry and clay shooting) and use it in the presence of either the occupier of private premises or persons authorised by them in writing. The following detailed criteria must be met; if they are not, then both borrower and lender commit offences:

- The borrower of a shotgun may be of any age. (Self-explanatory.)

- The lender must be aged 18 or older and have a certificate in respect of the shotgun. (Again self-explanatory.)

- The borrower must be in the presence of the lender, i.e. in sight and earshot. (See discussion below.)

- The use of a shotgun must comply with any conditions on the certificate held in respect of that shotgun. (This refers to the four statutory conditions.)

- The purpose of the loan is only for hunting animals, shooting game or vermin or shooting artificial targets. (This is very specific; any activity other than these three is not covered. Artificial targets cover a wide variety of objects including clay pigeons, tin cans on a fence or a balloon filled with helium.)

- The lender must be:
  a) a person who has the right to allow others to enter the premises for the purpose of hunting animals or shooting game or vermin, (the landowner or sporting tenant), or
  b) a person authorised by them in writing. ('In writing' would include an email or an SMS text.)

The term 'in the occupier's presence' merits some discussion. Again, there is no legal definition of this, but the Home Office Guide offers helpful advice at 7.8. 'The term "in the presence of" is not defined in law but is generally interpreted as being in sight or earshot'. To my knowledge this has only been tested once in court.

In 2011, Mathew Thomas was charged with being in illegal possession of a firearm when he borrowed his father's .22 rifle to shoot at rabbits in the garden out of an upstairs window. His father was directly below him in the drawing room at the time and knew that his son was shooting, having loaned him the rifle. The court found that although his father was not physically next to him in the same room, Mr Thomas Snr could exert influence on his son's use of the rifle because he could hear his shouted instructions. Accordingly, it concluded that he was in his father's presence and acquitted him.

The 11A exemption also applies to lending rifles but with the following distinctions.

The borrower of a rifle must be aged 17 or older. (This comes from the old Section 16 exemption, the so-called 'estate rifle' clause. It often catches people out in photographs posted in shooting magazines where a youngster is shown proudly posing with his first bag of bunnies shot with Dad's rifle. If he was under 17 when he did it, then both he and his father have broken the law.)

The use of a rifle must comply with any conditions on the certificate held in respect of that shotgun. (This refers to any police imposed discretionary condition as well as the four statutory ones.)

NB This exemption does not apply to other Section 1 firearms, e.g. a muzzle-loading revolver.

The Section 11(6) exemption remains unchanged. It allows a non-certificate holder to shoot artificial targets at a time and a place approved by the Chief Constable. This is the exemption that most established clay target grounds use. However, it is also used for game fairs, country shows and for charity shoots. Although the exemption is primarily used for clay targets, there is nothing to stop any other type of inanimate target, for example gas-filled balloons or tin cans, from being used. The exemption is not so tightly drawn as 11(5) and does not specify who may lend the gun or similar matters.

It is important to note that as a certificate holder, you cannot just lend your gun to anybody to use. Always make sure that you have complied with every part of the legal exemptions, otherwise you may find yourself in trouble.

Drink driving

Many people are surprised to learn that a conviction for drink-driving could affect their certificates. Anyone driving while under the influence of drink or drugs generally faces public disapprobation on the basis that their lack of personal control might injure or kill innocent people. It is naïve to think that this view would not extend to owning firearms.

Medical professionals have been asked to give factual information to inform the decision-making process since the early 1990s. The legal test for a firearm certificate is that the chief officer shall not grant one to a prohibited person, a person of unsound mind, intemperate habits or one unfitted by any reason to be entrusted with such a firearm. In addition the chief officer has to be satisfied that the applicant has good reason for possessing the firearm and can be permitted to have it in his possession without danger to public safety or to the peace. The legal test for a shotgun certificate is slightly different. A chief officer shall not grant one to a prohibited person, or to a person whom he believes cannot be permitted to have a shotgun in his possession without danger to the public safety or to the peace.

For one drink-driving (DD) conviction with a relatively low alcohol level and no aggravating factors, a warning letter is likely to be issued. Any further infractions within the life of the certificate will see its revocation. A single incident which features a high blood alcohol level or other aggravating factors will result in an instant revocation. For instance, driving at high speed down a narrow country lane while twice over the limit will be taken as an aggravating factor.

Two or more DDs that are relatively close together will most likely result in revocation. DDs are notified to the National Firearms Licensing Management System as they occur, allowing for instant action to be taken.

Evidence of alcohol or drug abuse may indicate that a person is unfit/unsuitable to possess a firearm due to the possible impairment of judgement and loss of self-control. The relevant case here is Luke v Little [1980] supported by Chief Constable of Essex v Peter Germain [1991]. An assessment will need to be made into the circumstances of each case. Usually, it will be a pattern of behaviour that causes concern but there may also be cases where one-off incidents will bring into question the fitness/unsuitability of somebody to possess firearms. In the case of Lubbock v Chief Constable of Lothian and Borders [2001], the Sheriff ruled that the revocation of a firearm and shotgun certificate following one drink-driving incident was justified given the individual's general attitude towards the offence.

In Luke, the certificate holder was prone to gross bouts of drunkenness which gave rise to the belief/concern that he might succumb to the violent use of a shotgun during one of these bouts. Germain concerned repeated drink-driving offences which it was felt demonstrated general irresponsibility and lack of self-control. Therefore the Chief Constable could take such factors into consideration in his revocation. Both were heard in courts of record that create an authority.

In Lubbock, the ruling was case-specific and a first-instance case which creates no precedent. As it was heard in Scotland, it might be also be argued that this was heard in a foreign court with no jurisdiction in England and Wales. However, this case may still carry a lot of weight as firearms law is not devolved to Westminster. The statement of the arresting officer to the effect that the Defendant was the 'drunkest person he had ever seen', probably did little to help his cause. The Defendant also showed no remorse for his actions which doubtless influenced the Sheriff in making the decision.

Always consider that prescription drugs may react adversely with alcohol and affect your ability to drive. Have a word with your doctor to check this. Don't forget that alcohol stays in the bloodstream for a long time and it is still possible to be over the limit in the morning after a heavy drinking session the night before.

On the subject of alcohol, Section 25 of the 1968 Act makes it an offence to sell or transfer any firearm or ammunition to any person you know or have reasonable cause to believe is drunk or of unsound mind.

Section 12 of the Licensing Act 1872 makes it an offence in England and Wales to be drunk in possession of a loaded firearm anywhere. The essence of this offence is that the firearm must be loaded. A similar offence exists in Scotland under Section 50 of the Civic Government (Scotland) Act 1982 where it is an offence to have a firearm while drunk in a public place. (It does not matter whether it is loaded or not.)

Armed trespass

In law, trespass (unlawful visiting of land or other premises) is a civil offence or tort, falling outside of the criminal law. However anyone who trespasses with a firearm commits a serious criminal offence. Section 20 of the Firearms Act 1968 provides that anyone who trespasses in a building or on land with a gun commits an offence. There is a defence to show that by doing so you had reasonable excuse but the onus is on you to prove it. (For the purposes of this section, 'land' includes land covered in water.)

Always be certain of the boundaries of land over which you are entitled to shoot. Carrying a sketch map or marked OS map is a good idea. An app on a mobile phone which used GPS would be invaluable too. While a genuine incident of mistakenly straying beyond your boundary would doubtless be accepted as a 'reasonable excuse', the law takes a dim view of armed trespass.

Sound moderators

Since the early twentieth century, devices have been produced which are designed to make guns quieter. They are properly known as 'sound moderators' but are often called silencers. They work by reducing the sound pressure level of a gun when it is fired by allowing the gases caused by the combustion of the powder to dissipate slowly. The bang that a gun makes is caused by rapidly expanding gases and if the bullet is travelling at more than the speed of sound, its supersonic crack. Sound moderators are simply tubes either fitted with a series of baffles or with a specially shaped interior which slows the gases down as they escape.

Although they are just accessories for firearms, they are still treated as a firearm in law (Section 57(1)(c) of the Firearms Act 1968). They take on the legal status of the firearm to which they are affixed, hence:

- Air rifle under 12 ft/lb – no certificate needed.

- Shotgun – shotgun certificate needed for the gun but not the moderator.

- Sporting rifle, Section 1 airgun or shotgun – firearm certificate needed for both the rifle and the moderator and subject to the 'good reason test'.

Moderators are not specific to a rifle's calibre. Most will cover a wide spectrum. Remember that although a moderator may fit a number of different rifles, it must be authorised for use on every one.

As sound moderators reduce noise – which is classed as a pollutant in itself – it is self-evident that a responsible person should fit one to his gun if it is practicable to do so. Moderators make the noise from a gun going off non-directional and so give the shooter an advantage over his quarry, especially when taking multiple shots at rabbits. They also protect the shooter's hearing and, because they add weight to a rifle, reduce its recoil and consequently enhance accuracy. It is not possible to supress the supersonic crack from high-velocity bullets as they travel through the air. That is why .22 cartridges designed for use with moderators produce sub-sonic velocities. While a moderator won't stop any super-sonic crack, it does tend to quieten the rifle's discharge noise significantly.

You do not need to have any authorisation for moderators that are going on shotguns or air rifles. You will need a variation for any moderator that you intend to fit on to a rifle. To save money, the variation is best requested at the same time that you apply for the variation for the rifle. Obviously you will need to give a 'good reason' for doing so and while this will vary with individual circumstances, reasons such as protecting your hearing or minimising disturbance from sound pollution are credible. If the rifle has an integral moderator fitted to it, you do not need separate authorisation. This is only necessary if it is a detachable accessory. (Broome v Walter [1989].)

While a moderator will protect your hearing, you should always wear hearing protection when using one.

Young people and firearms licensing

Guns in the hands of young people is always a thorny topic. People who shoot are keen to pass on their knowledge to their children and other youngsters, if they show an interest. Fundamentalist anti-gun groups regard this as anathema. There have been lots of scare-mongering stories in the press in recent years after the revelation that children as young as eight have been granted shotgun certificates. The journalists concerned either don't know, or have conveniently forgotten, that these certificates are only granted after due police process.

There is a very sensible concept embedded in English law that recognises that as a young person increases in years he also becomes more mature. Accordingly, the stringent restrictions imposed on very young people are relaxed progressively until they become adults.

For many young people, the grant of their first shotgun certificate is something of a 'rite of passage'. The young person who was been granted a certificate will be most unlikely to misbehave because he knows the consequence will be to lose it. Acquiring a certificate after a police interview is a beneficial experience which assists the young person to recognise his shooting as a privilege dependent on obeying the law and the safe and responsible use of firearms.

When making enquiries about a young applicant's circumstance, the chief officer will want to make enquiries of people with whom the young person routinely comes into contact, for example teachers, Scout or youth leaders, etc. However, in doing so, the special relationship of trust that ought to exist between teacher and pupil should not be prejudiced.

It might be argued that the grant of a certificate to a person under the age of 14 is the easiest decision a chief officer has to make because it does not allow the young person to use the firearm without supervision.

Young people and shotgun certificates

What the law says:

The Firearms Act 1968, imposes no minimum age for the grant of a shotgun certificate. The Act has been amended on several occasions since it became law and without change to this provision. Section 28 provides that a chief officer shall grant a shotgun certificate unless:

- The applicant is a prohibited person or
- The chief officer has reason to believe that he cannot be permitted to possess a shotgun without danger to the public safety or to the peace; or
- The Chief Officer believes the applicant has no good reason for possessing a shotgun. (Section 3 of the Firearms (Amendment) Act 1988 modified Section 28(1) of the 1968 Act to this effect.) The burden falls on the police to demonstrate that the applicant has no good reason rather than vice-versa.

Even if a young person is granted a shotgun certificate he is not allowed to use a shotgun without the supervision of an adult (21 years or older) until he/she is 15. This deals with any objections which might be based on concerns over the age of criminal responsibility. In the UK, the age of criminal responsibility is ten years.

A young person cannot buy or hire a shotgun or ammunition until he or she reaches the age of 18.

How the licensing process should work

Settled law requires that a chief officer must consider each case on its merits and from the standpoint of the applicant rather than from that of an objector. (Anderson v Neilans [1940], Joy v Chief Constable Dumfries and Galloway [1966].)

Chief officers are not allowed to have blanket policies, for example not granting certificates to under 12-year-olds. Any policy must not be punitive and must always admit of exceptions if it is to be lawful. (R v Wakefield Crown Court, ex parte Oldfield [1977].)

In considering an application, chief officers should apply the following criteria

- Is the young person of adequate stature to use a shotgun safely? (Obviously a small child who struggles to use a gun which is too large for him is potentially dangerous to himself and others.)

- Does he/she understand the basic rules of safe gun handling and can he demonstrate them? (The cardinal rule of safe gun handling is muzzle awareness i.e. the shooter should always know where the muzzle of his gun is in order to make sure that it does not point where damage or injury might result if it was to go off.)

- Will he/she receive proper support and training from his immediate social circle? (This is very important as the development in responsibility is generally linked to the support and trust conferred by others.)

If the answer to all of these questions is YES then the grant of a certificate to a young person poses no danger to public safety or to the peace.

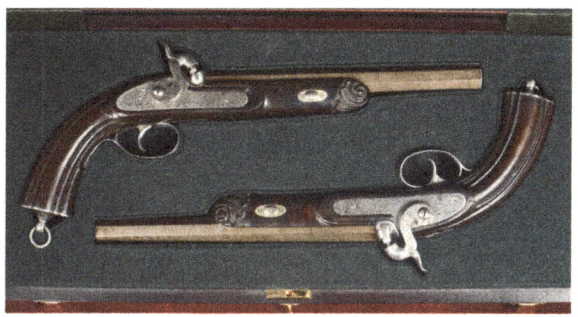

The official view

> 'It is in the interests of safety that a young person who is to handle firearms should be properly taught at a relatively early age.'

Home Office Guide on Firearms Licensing Law. Section 7.25

A senior judge's view

> 'We do not consider that the appellant's age is either directly or indirectly something likely to give rise to the public safety or to the peace.'

The remarks of Mr Justice Garland in Peter Burge v Chief Constable of Norfolk, December 1994.

LAW AND LICENSING • 55

The government's view

'As with many other issues, we believe that this is one on which parents should decide the age at which their children should take part in shooting sports.'

Charles Clark MP in the government's reply to the Home Affairs Committee Report *'Controls over Firearms'*. Cm 4864 October 2000 (Mr Clark, the then Home Secretary rejected the Committee's proposal that there should be a minimum age for handling any firearm, set at 12 or 14 years).

A senior police officer's view

In his evidence to the 2010 Home Affairs Committee inquiry Firearms Control, Assistant Chief Constable Adrian Whiting (then Association of Chief Police Officers (ACPO) lead, Firearms Licensing) said: 'The evidence in relation to young people shooting does not give any cause for concern.'

Mr Whiting was asked by the Chairman of the Home Affairs Committee for his opinion on the appropriate minimum age for a certificate:

Keith Vaz MP: Of course, but if you were looking at consolidating this and making it one age, so it is not confusing to members of this Committee and the public when they don't know at what age they can apply, what age would the ACPO lead on firearms suggest would be appropriate?

Adrian Whiting: The minimum age would be ten, I would suggest, Sir.

The age of criminal responsibility is ten years.

Young people and firearms

UNDER 14 YEARS OF AGE
No one under the age of 14 may use a Section 1 Firearm except for target shooting as a member of a Home Office approved rifle club; or at a shooting gallery where no rifles larger than .23 inch calibre are used (e.g. at fairs).

14 TO 17 YEARS OF AGE
At the age of 14 a person may hold a firearm certificate and may then be given firearms and ammunition within the conditions imposed by the police on the certificate.

The law does not set a minimum age at which the holder of a firearm certificate may shoot without adult supervision. That is left to the discretion of the parent or guardian.

18 AND OVER
On reaching the age of 18, the holder of a firearm certificate may hire or purchase firearms and ammunition in accordance with the conditions on that certificate.

Young people and shotguns

UNDER 15 YEARS OF AGE
In this age group if you hold a certificate you are only allowed to borrow a shotgun. There are two ways to do so: firstly for 72 hours according to certificate instructions (i.e. without completing any written transfer or notification to police), and secondly by written transfer by the lender onto table 2 of the recipients certificate and a notification to police by both parties (as per certificate instructions). You may not purchase, hire or be given a shotgun or ammunition.

15 TO 17 YEARS OF AGE
Between 15 and 17, with a certificate, you may be given or lent a shotgun (and cartridges) for up to 72 hours by another certificate holder to use on private premises without supervision.

Making a gift of a shotgun requires an adult (18 or older) to follow the instructions on his shotgun certificate. In practice this means conducting a full transfer of the shotgun by making an entry in table 2 of the young recipient's certificate stating the word 'gift' in the relevant box. Both the person giving and receiving the shotgun must then inform their own police licensing departments of the transaction within seven days by recorded delivery or by email to the email address designated by the issuing authority. Once you have been given a shotgun you may also lend your shotgun to other certificate holders for up to 72 hours without the need for a written transfer to be made. If you have to lend your shotgun for longer than 72 hours you must make an entry into table 2 of the borrower's certificate. Both the person transferring and receiving the shotgun must then inform their own police licensing departments of the transaction within seven days by recorded delivery or by email to the email address designated by the issuing authority. When the shotgun is returned to you; the same process applies but in reverse.

Age limits for possessing firearms and shotguns

As the law is very complicated about the ages when young people may possess certain firearms, the following table may be helpful.

	Under 18	Under 15	Under 14
Purchase or hire any firearm (including shotguns and air weapons) or ammunition	No	No	No
Possess a Section 1 firearm and ammunition	Yes	Yes	No (see exceptions 1, 2 & 3 below)
Receive a Section 1 firearm and ammunition as a gift	Yes	Yes	No
Possess assembled shotgun and ammunition	Yes	No (see exceptions 1, 4 & 5 below)	No (see exceptions 1, 4 & 5 below)
Receive a shotgun as a gift	Yes	No	No
Possess an air weapon	No (see exceptions 1, 2, 3, 4 & 6 below)	No (see exceptions 1, 2, 3, 4 & 6 below)	No (see exceptions 1, 2, 3 & 4 below)
Receive an air weapon as a gift	No	No	No
Possess an air weapon in a public place	No (see exceptions 1, 2, 3 & 4 below)	No (see exceptions 1, 2, 3 & 4 below)	No (see exceptions 1, 2, 3 & 4 below)

LAW AND LICENSING

Exceptions:

(1) If carrying on behalf of the certificate holder (who is aged 18 years or over) and for the certificate holder's sporting purposes only.

(2) When part of an approved club or cadet corps.

(3) On a miniature rifle range.

(4) Under the supervision of someone over 21 years old.

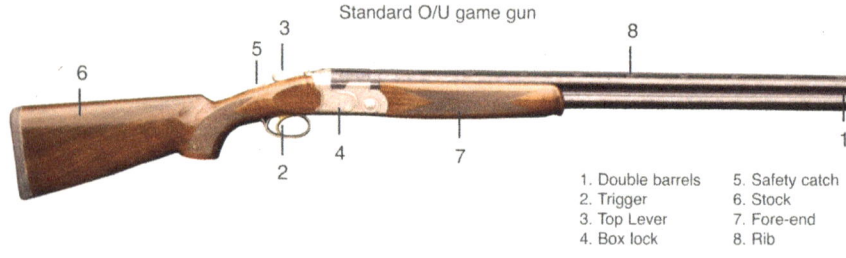

1. Double barrels
2. Trigger
3. Top Lever
4. Box lock
5. Safety catch
6. Stock
7. Fore-end
8. Rib

(5) When the shotgun is in a securely fastened gun cover so that it cannot be fired.

(6) Unless on private property with permission of the land owner. It is an offence for someone under this exception to fire any missile beyond the boundary of the premises unless with permission of the adjacent land owner.

Fees for certificates

The cost of the grant or renewal of a certificate (and other specified licensing related functions) are set by a Parliamentary Order which is amended periodically. (The details of the current Order are available on the Home Office website.) The following functions are not charged for:

- A replacement certificate for one that is full or dilapidated (but not for a lost one).

- An application to have a condition changed.

- The issue of a new certificate when you change address.

- The grant of a temporary permit.

- A variation for the increase of ammunition only.

- A one-for-one variation i.e. one which does not increase the number of firearms on the certificate.

Cartridges with expanding missiles (bullets)

The Policing and Crime Act 2017 repealed the 1997 prohibition on rifle cartridges with expanding missiles (bullets). However, pistol cartridges with expanding bullets are still classed

as prohibited ammunition under S 5(1A)(f). The test of whether a cartridge constitutes pistol ammunition is whether or not it was solely designed for use in pistols. For example, a .357 Magnum cartridge with a hollow-point bullet is not considered to be a pistol cartridge as many rifles are chambered for it. Cartridges loaded with expanding bullets may be used for target shooting.

In reality, there are only six pistol cartridges that are considered to be prohibited ammunition if loaded with expanding bullets. These are all relatively obscure and none of them have any relevance to quarry shooting.

Rifle cartridges loaded with expanding bullets are classed as Section 1 items and are subject to firearm certificate control.

Ballistic minima values for shooting deer

Legislation requires that cartridges used to shoot deer must conform to certain ballistic minima.

Red, sika and fallow deer

England & Wales	A minimum calibre of .240 with a muzzle energy of 1,700 foot-pound. The bullet must be soft or hollow nosed.
Scotland	A bullet of not less than 100 grs, driven at a muzzle velocity of not less than 2,450 fps producing a kinetic energy of not less than 1,750 ft lb. Bullets must be expanding and designed to deform in a predictable manner.

Roe deer

England & Wales	May not be shot with anything smaller than a .240 cal rifle with a muzzle energy of 1,750 ft lb.

Scotland   May be shot with a bullet of not less than 50 grs, driven at a muzzle velocity of not less than 2,450 fps producing a kinetic energy of not less than less than 1,000 ft lb.

Muntjac or Chinese water deer

England & Wales   May be shot with a rifle of not less than .22 calibre firing a soft or hollow nosed and developing a muzzle velocity of not less than 1,000 ft lb.

Scotland   Shotguns are generally regarded as being unsuitable and inhumane for shooting deer but the law allows them to be used in certain, very limited circumstances for agricultural crop protection.

Pistols for humane despatch

Although the Firearms (Amendment) Act 1997 banned most pistols from private ownership, Parliament saw fit to put a specific, special exemption for this purpose into the Act.

The exemption for pistols for humane despatch can be found at Section 3:

The authority of the Secretary of State is not required by virtue of Section (1)(aba) of Section 5 of the 1968 Act for a person to have in his possession, or to purchase or acquire or to sell or transfer, a firearm if he is authorised by a firearm certificate to have the firearm in his possession, or to purchase or acquire it, subject to a condition that it is only for use in connection with the humane killing of animals.

There are some sections within the firearms licensing community who believe that when Parliament prohibited pistols it applied to them all. This is not so. The test for owning a pistol for humane despatch is that you have to prove (the onus is on you) 'good reason'. This does not mean that you just fancy having one; neither does it mean that you have to show that you need one, for example for your job.

However, proving 'good reason' for pistols is never easy and must be substantial i.e. have substance about it. (It should be noted that 'substantial' does not necessarily mean volume but also includes a serious and genuine intention.)

You would have to give some form of evidence that you shot a significant number of deer each year (more than the average stalker) and that there were several occasions that you wounded deer and

that possessing a pistol was the only humane way of giving the coup de grâce. This is something of a double-edged sword as by saying that you had wounded a large number of deer, the police might brand you as incompetent with the rifle and thus a danger to public safety. Your certificate would be in danger of being revoked, with all the grief that goes with it.

There are times when a large volume deer stalker could satisfy the 'good reason' test. Perhaps the land over which he shot was very rocky making the use of a rifle at close range dangerous because of 'splashback'. (This is when the power from the rifle cartridge sends a cloud of material, for example stones, bone splinters or bullet fragments back towards the shooter.) Equally, there will be times in densely-forested country where the wounded deer has crawled into thick cover and it would be dangerous or impractical to pursue it while encumbered by a rifle.

If you are granted a pistol it will be a one or two shot .32 revolver, although a .38/.357 may be justified in the case of larger deer or boar. You will not be granted a self-loading pistol as their magazines cannot be effectively restricted and they are dangerous if permanently fixed in place. This is confirmed by Paragraph 12.38 of the Guide which says:

'Police forces should note that self-loading (semi-automatic) handguns should not be authorised for the slaughter or humane destruction of animals as it is not possible to permanently adapt the capacity of handguns which make use of a removable magazine.'

You will not be granted a self-loading pistol as their magazines cannot be effectively restricted and they are dangerous if permanently fixed in place. Your certificate will be conditioned to restrict the use to humane killing and if your 'good reason' was land related it may limit its use to that land. Thus applying for one because you really only fancied a bit of impromptu target shooting in the woods won't wash.

It is important to note that you do not have to be professionally involved with the humane killing of animals for example, a vet or terrier man to be granted a variation. Neither are you required to have successfully completed a course for their use, if indeed there are any.

The application for the grant of a firearm certificate variation for a pistol for humane despatch must be genuine, evidence-led and should only be made after mature consideration.

Antique firearms

In December 2015, the Law Commission published its report *Firearms Law Reforms to Address Pressing Issues*. Chapter 4 was dedicated to examining how antique firearms were dealt with as part of the wider

Firearms Act 1968. The Commission recommended that the term 'antique firearm' be defined in law and also how this should be based on age and functionality.

The government accepted this recommendation and brought forward legislation to achieve it. Section 126 of the Policing and Crime Act 2017 modified Section 58(2) of the Firearms Act 1968. This Section provides that:

> 'nothing in this Act relating to firearms shall apply to an antique firearm which is sold, transferred, purchased, acquired or possessed as a curiosity or ornament'.

This is the basic exemption whereby people are allowed to possess antique firearms without them being subject to the firearms licensing regime and all that goes with it. It was imported (almost verbatim) from Section 13 of the Firearms Act 1920. No definition was provided as to what constituted an antique firearm. In interpreting this term, the courts used the normal meaning, i.e. something having age or from olden times. This led to the courts finding some older firearms to be antiques when the Home Office guidance recommended that they should not benefit from the Section 58(2) exemption. (The most celebrated (or notorious) instance of this was a court finding that a 9mm British Lanchester submachine gun made during World War Two, was an antique firearm.)

On 1 March 2021, the policing minister issued new Regulations which defined the term 'antique firearm'. These are *The Antique Firearms 2021*.

Regulation 1 deals with the citation and commencement of the Regulations etc.

The commencement date for the Regulations was 22 March 2021.

Regulation 2 lists the obsolete cartridges in the Schedule attached to the Regulations.

The Schedule is closely based on the so-called Obsolete Calibres list from the *Home Office Guide on Firearms Licensing Law, 2016*. It contains a large number of imperial and metric centre-fire cartridges for breech-loading long arms and pistols as well as shotgun cartridges for vintage rifles, punt guns and shotguns.

The Schedule does not include seven centre-fire revolver cartridges which were on the Home Office Obsolete Calibre list, namely:

.320 British
9.4mm Dutch
10.6mm German
11mm French (M1873) Army
.41 Colt (both Long and Short)
.442 (often called .44 Webley)
.44 Smith & Wesson Russian

These cartridges were excluded because of the increasing level of attractiveness to criminals of pistols which used them as well as the ease of manufacture of suitable ammunition. People who owned revolvers chambered for these cartridges can continue to own them as Section 7(1) Historic firearms on the authority of a firearm certificate.

Regulation 3 lists the propulsion systems of firearms defined as antiques.
(The term propulsion system is more properly ignition system.)

(a) any propulsion system which involves the use of a loose charge and a separate ball (or other missile) loaded at the muzzle end of the barrel, chamber or cylinder of the firearm and which uses an independent source of ignition.

This encompasses any muzzle-loading firearm (including revolvers). Matchlocks, wheellocks snaphaunces, flintlocks and any form of chemical percussion ignition whether detonating powder, percussion cap, patch lock, tube primer, etc.

(b) any propulsion system in a breech-loading cartridge firearm which uses an ignition system other than rim-fire or centre-fire.

This covers capping breech-loaders, needle fire (both long and short needle) and pinfire ignition.

(c) any propulsion system which involves the use of rim-fire cartridges (other than .22 (5.58mm), .23 (5.8mm), 6mm or 9mm rim-fire cartridges) in a breech-loading firearm)

.22 & 9mm RF cartridges are still in common use. .23 or 6mm RF cartridges are so dimensionally similar to .22RF as to be indistinguishable and interchangeable.

(d) any propulsion system for an air weapon. Spring, bellows, reservoir, etc.

Regulation 4 specifies the date of manufacture for an antique firearm. This is 1 September 1939 (the invasion of Poland by the Third Reich). Any firearm manufactured after this date can **never** be an antique firearm. Consequently, modern replicas of muzzle-loading, and other antique firearms can only be possessed on the authority of a firearm or shotgun certificate.

Whilst the 2021 Regulations import clarity and thus certainty into Section 58(2) of the Firearms Act by defining the term 'antique firearm', any firearm which meets the terms of the definition still has to be sold, purchased, possessed or acquired as a curiosity or ornament in order for the exemption to be claimed.

Ornament is quite easy to define. The Shorter Oxford English Dictionary (SOED) says: 'Something used to adorn, beautify or embellish; a decoration, an embellishment, esp a small trinket, vase, figure, etc.' An

old muzzle-loading shotgun from the 1860s, which is hung over the fireplace, is indubitably an ornament. However, an ornament does not necessarily have to be on display. This is a subjective test, and it is the owner's intent that is important.

Defining 'a curiosity' is slightly more problematic as this is even more subjective. *SOED* gives 'Scientific or artistic interest; connoisseurship'. Curiosity has to have interest or inquisitiveness as an ingredient.

Irrespective of the niceties of defining the term 'curiosity or ornament', one thing is clear; it does not extend to using the firearm.

If you want to fire an antique firearm, then it needs to be covered by the relevant certificate. If the antique gun is a Section 1 firearm, then you will have to satisfy the 'good reason' test at Section 27 of the Firearms Act 1968 as with any other. However, the Home Office recognises that there are some antique collectors who only want to fire their guns occasionally. This is catered for by Sections 8.14 &15 of the *Guide on Firearms Licensing Law*.

Occasional firing

8.14 An antique firearm can only be held as a curiosity or ornament and cannot be fired. However, they can be added to a firearm or shotgun certificate for the purposes of collection and occasional firing. Where the 'good reason' for possession is collection and not target shooting, Section 44 of the Firearms (Amendment) Act 1997 requiring membership of a club to be named on the certificate is not applicable. Where a person has an antique firearm which they wish to fire for test, research, re-enactment, target shooting or competition purposes, no test of frequency of use should be applied when assessing good reason to possess: the primary reason for possession will be collection.

8.15 An antique firearm may be brought onto a certificate or removed from time to time or when there is a change of ownership. A signed statement of intent by the owner to the local police firearms licensing department should be sufficient to effect the necessary change of status when required. A variation fee would become payable where an 'antique' is brought onto a certificate to allow it to be fired, unless a 'one for one' variation is sought. In the latter case, it should be borne in mind that mostly only mass-produced muzzle-loading arms had standardised bore sizes. Therefore, a variation for a craft-made muzzle-loader may require finding a suitable example before the calibre can be ascertained. As this may take some time, some latitude may be given over the time taken for such 'one for one' variations.

If you have an antique firearm on certificate, then there is no reason why you should not have it removed from the certificate if you no longer wish to shoot it. All that is necessary is for you to inform (not ask) the licensing department that this is the case. The letter needn't be complicated and should go something like this:

'It is no longer my intention to shoot the 54-bore Tranter revolver No. 123456 on my firearm certificate. Henceforth, I shall keep it as a curiosity or ornament and have removed it from my certificate. Please amend your records accordingly.'

The police cannot refuse to allow you to do this although they may want to satisfy themselves that the firearm is a real antique.

It should be noted that the antique exemption only applies to firearms and not their ammunition, which has the same legal status as if it were a modern cartridge. Indeed, possession of modern, viable ammunition with an indisputably antique firearm may call the quality of possession of it into question. That said, there will be instances where collectors of antique firearms may have suitable ammunition for their guns quite legitimately, for example:

- Original paper cartridges and percussion caps for a P1853 Enfield rifle musket.
- Original self-contained cartridges for a Prussian M1862 Dreyse needle rifle
- Original pinfire shot cartridges for a LeFauchex shotgun.
- Original metal foil cartridges and percussion caps for a US Civil War Smith carbine.

Possession of inert cartridges or dummies to show the functionality of an antique firearm's action does not prejudice a claim that it is kept as a curiosity or ornament.

Some collectors/shooters may hold firearm certificates that refer to an otherwise antique firearm and suitable ammunition for it. That does not prevent such individuals from owning similar types of firearms without a certificate under the Section 58(2) exemption. For example, a certificate holder may have an indifferent condition .577/450 Martini-Henry rifle and ammunition for shooting in addition to three other Martinis in good condition that are not shot but held as antiques. The lawful possession of the ammunition in no way calls the quality of possession of the three antique rifles into question. The intent is all-important.

Owners of antique firearms who rely on the 58(2) exemption should do nothing that calls their reason for possessing them into question. The exemption does not change the legal status of the firearms, it simply disapplies it so long as the requirement to keep them as 'curiosities or ornaments' continues to be met. Thus, an 8mm Austrian Roth-Steyr pistol will always have the status of a prohibited small firearm under Section 5(1)(aba) of the Firearms Act 1968.

Don't forget that unlawful possession of a prohibited weapon attracts a mandatory five-year custodial sentence.

Prohibited persons

There is the concept in law that someone who has been convicted of a serious offence that merited a prison sentence should not be able to possess firearms or ammunition, including air guns and antique firearms. This includes people who were given a custodial sentence that was suspended by the judge.

Section 21 of the 1968 Act imposes a prohibition from owning any firearm or ammunition for five years on anyone who has been sentenced to more than three months but less than two years. In cases where the sentence is greater than two years then the prohibition is for life. Where the Judge suspends the sentence, then prohibition is for five years from the second day after the date upon which sentence was passed.

It is also an offence to supply a firearm or ammunition to a person they know to be prohibited. On, that basis, it is always a good idea to ask anyone that you do not know well whether or not they are prohibited. I understand that when a person is released from prison they are told about the provision and sign a declaration to say they understand it. You should not be worried about causing any offence by asking the question as you are entitled to protect your own position and you do not want to be put in the situation where it might be alleged that you deliberately broke the law. It is better that someone is offended than you are imprisoned.

If you are running a clay shoot under Section 11(6) exemption where complete strangers might want a go, then you should make them sign a declaration that they are not prohibited. If they won't sign, then they don't shoot. Simple.

It is possible to appeal to the Crown Court and ask a judge to lift the prohibition. You will have to persuade the court that you are a suitable person to be granted a certificate in spite of your antecedents. One really good character witness who will give evidence on your behalf is essential. The Chief Constable is entitled to put his side of the story and then the judge decides. If the prohibition is lifted, then the Chief Constable still has to decide whether or not you are suitable to be granted a certificate.

Air weapons

In law, all air guns are considered to be 'firearms'. This may sound a contradiction in terms but if you consider that all guns expel their missiles by means of a compressed gas then it is not as illogical as it may sound. In the case of air weapons, the compressed gas is air rather than the products of rapid chemical reaction. Having established that air guns are 'firearms', it then follows that, in principle, any legislative provision of the Firearms Acts applies to them. For example, it is an offence to offer 'unlawful violence' (threaten) with an air rifle as it is with a shotgun.

Air weapons are the only firearms in law which are controlled by their 'power' (actually kinetic energy) output. Low-powered air weapons – not those defined as being 'specially dangerous' are generally only controlled by age and are not part of the firearms licensing process. The Firearms (Dangerous Air Weapons) Rules, 1969 provide that an air pistol which produces a kinetic energy level in excess of 6 ft lb is deemed 'specially dangerous' as is any other air weapon which generates 12 ft lb or more. In the case of a specially dangerous air weapon it is a prohibited firearm and in the case of an air gun, subject to Section 1 or 2 and a firearm or shotgun certificate.

Kinetic energy is a function of velocity and pellet mass divided by a gravitational constant. The formula is velocity squared X pellet mass (in grains) divided by a constant of 450420. Alternatively you can use ½ MV². The resulting value is in ft lb. In any prosecution for an over-powered air gun the Crown should be placed on strict liability to prove that when the suspect air gun was in the Defendant's possession it was over the limit. Storage conditions which have allowed oil to seep into the air compression chamber may have contributed to the phenomenon of 'dieseling' which causes increased power yields. The oil when combined with the air produces a fuel/air mixture which is ignited by the friction of the air being compressed. The resulting combustion produces more gas and the pellet exits with greater speed.

Changing the pellet weight may cause an air rifle to go over the limit and any test regime should always comprise three bands of pellet range, the heaviest and lightest possible and the mid-range weight. For an air rifle to be deemed to exceed the power limit, it should do this routinely with a pellet from each of the band weights rather than just occasionally with one extreme weight.

It goes without saying that anything done deliberately to raise the power limit of an air rifle past the 12 ft lb level is wholly illegal and puts you in danger of prosecution and all the grief – expense, risk to reputation and your certificate – that accompanies this unhappy state. Be very circumspect about changing springs as a different brand may put the air rifle over the limit. Equally, fiddling with the mechanism of a precharged pneumatic is never advisable.

Due to an unintended consequence in the law, once an air rifle with a barrel under 24 inches (i.e. most of them) has been converted to an FAC-rated air rifle, it can never revert to just being an ordinary air rifle again (Firearms (Amendment) Act Section 7(2)(a)). In my personal opinion, FAC-rated air rifles are not worth the time, trouble and expense they entail. If you are applying for one then you might as well go the whole hog and apply for a .22 rifle. Should there be a safety consideration about using a full strength .22 cartridge in a situation where damage might occur, then consider using a .22 CB long cartridge. They will feed in bolt-action rifles as they are dimensionally similar to the .22 Long Rifle. However, they have a lighter bullet and a much reduced powder charge which produces only about 30 ft lb of kinetic energy as opposed to the most powerful, hyper-velocity cartridges which produce a staggering 190 ft lb. Generally, the CB Long will not function in a self-loading rifle.

Relevant component parts of guns

The Policing and Crime Act 2017 amended Section 57 of the Firearms Act 1968 to define a relevant component part. Section

57(1)(c) refers to 'relevant component parts', whilst S 57(1)D defines them thus:

For the purposes of subsection (1)(c), each of the following items is a relevant component part in relation to a lethal barrelled weapon or a prohibited weapon –

- (a) a barrel, chamber or cylinder,
- (b) a frame, body or receiver,
- (c) a breech block, bolt or other mechanism for containing the pressure of discharge at the rear of a chamber, but only where the item is capable of being used as a part of a lethal barrelled weapon or a prohibited weapon.

The parts of a shotgun (Section 2) are not considered to be 'shotguns' in their own right. Consequently a spare pair of barrels does not have to be entered onto your shotgun certificate (there is nowhere to do this anyway).

If you need to replace any component part of a Section 1 firearm, for example a rifle barrel, you do not need a variation to do so, but the dealer from whom you order the component part will want to satisfy himself that you have authority to possess it and will retain the old one for disposal.

Accessories for firearms such as telescopic sights are not component parts. Chamber reducing inserts/liners that allow different cartridges to be fired from the same gun are not either (Home Office Guide 2.61 (l)). This is entirely logical as the gun will still fire without them so, therefore, they cannot be parts.

There are some rifles built on the modular system with interchangeable bolts and barrels that enable different cartridges to be fired from what is in reality only one firearm. Each new barrel/bolt component requires a variation as they are all relevant component parts.

Crown Court appeals

There is the provision for anyone who is aggrieved by the decision of a Chief Constable to refuse to grant/renew/vary or to revoke a certificate to go the Crown Court (Section 44) and appeal against that decision. The court sits in the Chief Constable's stead and settled law (Rodenhurst v Chief Constable of Grampian [1992]) requires it to consider the matter anew and not just by way of review.

Crown Courts normally hear criminal matters but have inherited this function from the old Quarter Sessions. The appeal is really administrative law and the judge will normally sit with two lay magistrates. There is no jury as nobody is on trial. By the same token, the normal rules of evidence that should be admitted do not apply and the court may be given hearsay evidence and may afford it whatever weight it decides. Effectively there is a dual burden of proof. The Chief Constable (called the Respondent) must show that his decision to refuse to grant/renew/revoke was correct and the aggrieved party (called the Appellant) must show that he is a suitable person to have a certificate.

Both sides are normally represented by barristers although an Appellant-in-Person has the right of audience if he chooses to represent himself. (There is an old legal saying that someone who represents himself has a rogue for a lawyer and a fool for a client; I could not possibly comment). In my experience, HM Judges are fair and courteous people who will do their utmost to help an Appellant-in-Person so far as they are able. Certainly, a judge will not tolerate any bullying or hectoring by the Respondent's counsel of the appellant if he is not legally represented. He will also ask any questions that he thinks any police witness ought to be asked if the Appellant (who is not a professional advocate) does not ask them. Expert evidence may be called by either side if the Judge agrees.

Crown Court appeals are costly and uncertain affairs that nobody should enter into without mature consideration. An Appellant who loses an appeal is very likely to have an order for costs made against him and that can be very expensive. However, the converse is not true. An Appellant who wins will seldom recover his costs. Generally, costs are said 'to follow the fact', but they don't where firearms licensing appeals are concerned. This is a public policy matter and there is settled law which says that as the Chief Constable is exercising a public function for the good of society, he should not be penalised in costs if that decision is over-turned. The judge would have to find that the Chief Constable acted in a capricious manner in the way he made his decision if he was to order costs.

Mounting a Crown Court appeal is really an admission by both parties that they have failed to resolve the matter. Negotiation and reasonable compromise is always the best (and cheapest) course of action. Statistically, the odds of winning at Crown Court are about four to one against and that is with a good case that perhaps turns on some technical or procedural matter. Where the matter involves the Appellant's suitability and perhaps medical evidence will be called, then the odds rise dramatically to about ten to one against.

The Covid-19 pandemic has created massive backlogs in the courts. Listing officers rightly give precedence to criminal cases rather the administrative ones. Consequently, expect a very long wait for your case to be heard.

What constitutes a public place?

Much firearms law makes it an offence to do something in a 'public place'. This includes any highway and any other premises or place to which the public have or are permitted to have access at the material time whether on payment or otherwise (Section 57 (4)). Each case will be a matter of fact and degree. This has an especial bearing on land where there is the 'right to roam' under the Countryside and Rights of Way Act 2000. By way of example, the following would be considered to be public places:

- A game or country fair
- A clay target ground
- The area in front of the counter of a gun shop
- A public house
- A road or footpath (Obviously there are parts of these venues which are not public places).

The following are definitely **NOT** public places:

- Farm land where a game shoot is being held.
- A shooting club for members only
- Your garden.

The Royal Society for the Prevention of Cruelty to Animals

The RSPCA was founded for very laudable reasons and does much good work protecting domestic animals that are subject to the most dreadful abuse. However, RSPCA inspectors do not have the same powers as the police. Generally they do not have any statutory right of entry to your premises and cannot demand to inspect any part of them unless they are acting as a designated 'inspector' for the purposes of the Animal Welfare Act 2006.

In any other circumstances, if an RSPCA Inspector enters your premises without your permission they commit a trespass like anybody else. Despite the uniform, they do not have any special powers to conduct searches, gather evidence nor to confiscate your property. The RSPCA does not have any statutory powers in relation to firearms licensing.

Knives

Everyone I know who takes their recreation in the countryside carries a knife because it is an indispensable tool, for example, a deer stalker with a gralloching knife or a pigeon shooter with a machete to build his hide. However, there are some sections of the police who have the black-and-white mindset that all knives are bad and that nobody can carry them in public as they are dangerous, offensive weapons. (Most knife crime takes place with small kitchen knives. They tend to be very sharp, have flexible blades that go around bones and are available from the average kitchen drawer or supermarket.) With that in mind, it is as well to know what the law allows when carrying a knife.

The main principle is that most knives are not offensive weapons per se i.e. they have a peaceful use. Something like a Fairburn-Sykes commando dagger would probably be an offensive weapon per se as it has no other function than that of killing people. The courts have ruled that the following objects are not offensive weapons per se:

- A machete
- A sheath knife
- A cut-throat razor
- A clasp knife.

Generally, for something to be an offensive weapon, it has to be made with that sole purpose in mind or adapted for it. In the latter case intent has to be proven.

Section 139 of the Criminal Justice Act 1988 governs the carrying of knives in public. It is an offence for a person to have with him in a public place any article which has a blade or is sharply pointed. There are three specific statutory defences to this if a defendant can show that he had the article with him for:

Use at work (This would only cover someone who was actually using the knife as part of his job or who was travelling to or from work.)

For religious reasons (e.g. a Sikh who had a kirpan in his turban.)

As part of any national costume (e.g. the sgian dubh in a Scotsman's hose top or a jambiyah in Arab dress.)

It is also a statutory defence to prove (the onus lies on you) that you had the article in public with good reason or lawful authority. Good reason will be defined by the defendant's personal circumstances and at the time and place where he was charged. For example, a deer stalker would have good reason for having a hunting knife on his belt in a newsagent's on his way home from stalking. However, he would not have reasonable excuse for carrying it in a disco three days later. Any defence offered must be linked to the place where the article was carried.

Forgetfulness that you still possessed the knife sometime after its use is not a defence. On that basis it is always a good idea to search shooting coat pockets very thoroughly after carrying a knife if the coat is to be worn anywhere else. The same apples to your car.

The is also a statutory defence (Section 193(5)) for carrying a folding pocket knife in a public place so long as its blade or cutting edge is no longer then three inches or its metric equivalent (76.2mm). In order for the article to qualify as a folding knife it must be capable of folding at all times (DPP v Harris & DPP v Fehmi [1993]). This does include a lock knife but equally – contrary to what many police officers imagine – they are not prohibited as a result. Anyone who carries a locking knife in a public place must show good reason for doing so. The 'good reason' that immediately springs to mind is that you are carrying a knife with a locking blade in order to protect your fingers in case it closed on them during use.

There are several makes of specialist skinning knives that at first blush may appear to contravene the Criminal Justice Act 1988 (Offensive Weapons Order 1988) in that they are 'push daggers' (e.g. the Outdoor Edge Game Skinner). True, their blades protrude between two fingers while their specially shaped handles are grasped in a clenched fist just like a push dagger. However they fail the definition as they were made to be game-butchery tools and not weapons. (The definition says 'the weapon sometimes known as a "push dagger"'.) The reason they are made with this type of handle is to allow the user to retain his grip with bloody hands and ensures his safety while butchering. The same goes for specialist knives with finger holes in the handle, for example, the American Hunter Trophy Skinner. They are not knuckledusters as well.

Social media and firearm licensing

Be very careful about what you post onto social media. Irrespective of the controls you think you may have installed nothing that you put onto Facebook or Twitter is private any more. What you think is an innocent picture may reveal the location of where your guns are kept and leave you open to the accusation of irresponsible behaviour. A picture may also disclose an offence has happened.

Here are three examples:

- A man allowed two of his pals to have their photos taken holding his guns. Unfortunately, one of them had a record for football hooliganism and was well known to the police. It did not help that this individual posted comments to the effect that he wished he could take the guns to the next game and sort out opposing supporters with them. The owner's certificate was revoked on the strength of that.

- A young man posted a picture of himself in just his underpants while holding what appeared to be an empty vodka bottle and his gun on a website which encouraged people to drink a bottle of spirits with great rapidity. Unsurprisingly, the chief officer took the view that he was a person of 'intemperate habits' and revoked his certificate.

- In order to promote his business as a shooting guide, a man posted a video on YouTube of some of his clients shooting ducks. The only problems with that were that they were a) shooting over land that he did not have permission to shoot on and b) one of his clients was a prohibited person with a history of domestic violence. (He failed to make the right enquiries before agreeing to take him shooting.) His certificate was revoked and the client who was prohibited was sent down.

Be equally wary of posting on forums. I have rarely seen a sensible discussion on a forum. They all seem to degenerate very quickly into slanging matches between trolls. You don't want to be recognised as a participant in one of these vitriolic exchanges. What you said in jest, in the heat of the moment when perhaps you might have had a bit too much to drink may suddenly become taken as a threat to cause harm that will lose you your guns. I have seen it happen.

Don't believe everything posted on a forum. If you want the answer to any shooting question go to the technical or legal staff at an association of which you are a member and don't trust to the pronouncements of ignorant, self-opinionated amateurs. They will probably get you into trouble.

Personally speaking, I think social media is potentially more trouble than it is worth. That said, we should all be proud of our shooting achievements and experiences and should not be shy about telling others. You need to find the balance between discretion and expressing pride in your sport on social media.

Transfer of firearms

It is an inherent and very important part of the licensing regime that the acquisition or disposal of a firearm or shotgun has to be notified to the police in order to create an 'audit trail' and to ensure that the police licensing database is kept up to date. Notifications are very important and you can expect to be prosecuted if the police can prove that you have not done so. Conviction normally carries a hefty fine and in aggravated circumstances, a jail sentence.

Consequently, when you acquire a firearm or a shotgun you must tell the Chief Constable who issued your certificate that you have done so within seven days. This need not be very complicated and these days, it can be done by email to the address that your Firearms Licensing Department nominates (usually on the force website). You need to tell the police the following details.

- The calibre or bore of the gun
- The make and model (if it has one)
- The type e.g. double-barrelled shotgun or bolt-action rifle
- The serial number (if it has one)
- Where you got it from, e.g. Registered Firearms Dealer, North Wales Police, no.125
- The nature of the transaction e.g. sale, gift, loan, etc.
- The date of the transaction.

Quite a few guns do not have serial numbers. You should resist any calls by the police to have one stamped or engraved on your gun simply to facilitate police record keeping.

The same applies if you get rid of a gun, permanently. Giving a gun to a dealer for a repair does not have to be notified, although it is sensible to have a receipt for it. The same applies to someone who consigns a gun to a firm of auctioneers or asks a gun dealer to sell it on commission. You do not have to notify the police until it actually sells.

When you send a notification always keep a copy of it. Print off the email or keep a copy of the letter and the Recorded Delivery slip. Remember, you do not have to prove that you sent the notification; it is for the police to prove that you did not. However, if you have proof that you made the notification, you immediately hold the moral high ground. Police forces are big organisations; letters get lost and clerks forget to update databases.

There is no statutory form for making a notification, but BASC offers one on its website. Many police forces helpfully offer a localised variation of it which can be downloaded and printed off.

The 72-hour rule

Section 33 of the Firearms (Amendment) Act 1997 permits the loan of a shotgun to another certificate holder for no more than 72 hours without the need to notify the police. This is a very valuable facility which allows the temporary short-term loan of a gun. The loan can be extended for as many periods of 72 hours as the parties to the loan may decide. Both parties do not actually have to be physically present when the loan period is extended; an extension by Skype, email, text or telephone is perfectly legal. In such cases there will be evidence of the extension. Someone who simply lends a shotgun to another person and then they both forget about it are likely to find themselves in trouble if the police question its whereabouts.

The law is silent on whether or not the 72-hour rule can be used by a Registered Firearms Dealer to allow a certificate holder client to borrow a shotgun from his stock to try it out. In the absence of any negative court ruling, I take the view that it is lawful to do so.

Dual ownership of firearms and shotguns

There is nothing in law that says that one gun may not appear on multiple certificates. Certainly, people who live and shoot together find it a very convenient arrangement. It does have a potential downside in that if the gun is ever lost or stolen then everyone upon whose certificate it appears stands in theoretical danger of revocation or prosecution. Also, they are potentially liable to have to serve notices of acquisition or transfer. However, the reality is that the National Firearms Licensing System database recognises a 'principal holder' who is regarded as having responsibility for the gun. If it were to be lost or stolen then that person would be the subject of a normal police investigation to establish the facts. The person who possessed it at the time would face any allegations of liability.

Where Section 1 firearms are concerned, it is possible to ask for a condition that allows you to use the firearms on another person's certificate. For example, let's assume there are two chaps – Smith and Jones – who want to use the same rifle for fox control on the same estate. The certificate of Mr Jones could be conditioned to allow him to use the .223 rifle and ammunition that appears on Mr Smith's certificate. Obviously Mr Jones would have to satisfy the 'good reason' test in the same way as if he were applying for his own rifle. If you think this arrangement might benefit you, speak to your local Firearms Licensing Manager and talk it over.

If you decide to share a gun which is also on another person's certificate then make sure you know which of you actually has it. I have heard of horror stories where two people who shared a gun and neither knew who had it. That is not a happy situation and certainly not one in which to find yourself.

Shotgun cartridges

Unlike rifle (or other bulleted ammunition) shotgun cartridges do not have to be entered onto your certificate and do not have to be stored securely. (It is common sense to secure them against inquisitive children and they should not be left lying about as their theft inevitably gets the shooting community a bad name.)

To qualify as a shotgun cartridge, a cartridge must be under two inches in diameter and be loaded with at least five shot none of which exceeds .36 inch in diameter. This equates to UK 'LG' buckshot or to US 000 Buck. A firearm certificate is needed to lawfully possess shotgun cartridges loaded with a solid slug, for example Brenneke.

No authority is needed in the UK to possess shotgun cartridges by persons over 18. However, it is necessary to show your shotgun certificate at the time of purchase. It is possible to give an authority in writing to another person (over 18) to purchase shotgun cartridges on your behalf providing they have your shotgun certificate as well.

Guns and violence

It goes without saying that it is a very serious offence to use a gun (whether loaded or not) to threaten another person. This applies to air rifles, deactivated firearms and toys. Do not be tempted to do it, no matter how desperate the situation may be. At best you are highly likely to have your certificate(s) revoked and face prosecution; at worst you will be shot by armed police.

There is a common law right to self-defence but the use of a firearm to threaten could only be justified if you genuinely feared for your life and there was no other reasonable alternative (reasonable force). Having said that, such a course of action can never be advised, as the person who is threatened will simply report you to the police, with all the grief that entails.

It is an offence to possess any firearm with intent to endanger life or to cause fear in another person that unlawful violence may be used against him or another person. A conviction carries the maximum penalty of ten years in jail.

No matter what people on internet forums may say about civil rights, this is a matter of last resort. Beware the counsel of barrack-room lawyers. IGNORANTIA LEX NON EXCUSAT!

Index - Sporting Firearms - Law and Licensing

A
address changes 23–4, 61
age restrictions 38, 52–6, 57–8
air weapons 38, 42, 43, 50, 51, 59, 69, 73, 74–6
alcohol abuse 13, 16, 18, 48–9
ammunition 21, 30, 32, 40, 61–2, 72–3
Anti–Social Behaviour Act 2003 38, 42
antique firearms 66–73
appeals 78–9
applying for certificates 7–10
armed trespass 49–50
artificial targets 45, 46

B
BASC (British Association for Shooting and Conservation) 7, 14, 41
buildings, proximity to 36–7

C
cabinets 26–9, 34
certificates see firearm certificates; shotgun certificates
changes of address 23–4, 61
Civic Government (Scotland) Act 1982 49
collectors/collecting guns 9–10
component parts of guns 76–7
convictions 47–8, 85, 89
Criminal Justice Act 1988 81
Crown Court appeals 78–9
custodial sentences 73

D
deactivation of firearms 23, 88
deer 62–6
destruction of firearms 23
drink driving 47–9
dual ownership 87

E
England 49, 62, 63
expanding ammunition 5, 40, 61–2

F
falling shot 37–8
firearm certificates (FAC)
 appeals 78–9
 applying for 7–8, 10, 47, 50
 carrying 41–2
 conditions of 23–6
 dual ownership 80–81
 legal exemptions 44–7
 medical conditions 13–14, 18
 replacements 39, 61
 transfer of ownership 85–6
 young people 53

Firearms Act 1968
  antique firearms 66–7
  armed trespass 49–50
  carrying your certificate 41–2
  drink driving 47–9
  'good reason' 8–9, 10, 50, 51, 64, 66, 70, 71, 82, 87
  humane despatch 64–6
  legal exemptions 45, 46–7
  prohibited persons 73–4
  public places 79–80
  replacement certificates 39
  shotgun certificates 45, 46
  temporary permits 30–41
  young people 52–3
Firearms (Amendment) Act 1988 53
Firearms (Amendment) Act 1997 64, 71, 86
Firearms (Dangerous Air Weapons) Rules 1969 75
Firearms Enquiry Officers 10, 19
Firearms Security Handbook (Home Office) 30
footpaths, proximity to 36–7
Four Ds (security measures) 28
'freedom under the law' 8

G
game shooting, certificate exemptions 10, 44
'good reason' 8–9, 10, 50, 51, 64, 66, 70, 71, 82, 87
Guide on Firearms Licensing Law (Home Office) 8, 12, 55, 67
gun bearers/loaders 44
guns, componentry 76–7

H
Highways Act 1980 36
hiring, age restrictions 53, 57–8
Home Affairs Committee 2010 7, 56
Home Office
  Firearms Security Handbook 30
  Guide on Firearms Licensing Law see *Guide on Firearms Licensing Law*
hotels 34
humane despatch 64–6

I
imitation firearms 42

K
kinetic energy 37–8, 62, 63, 75, 76
knives 81–3

L
Licensing Act 1872 49
livestock 36
loaded weapons 42, 43, 49
loss of firearms 23

M
medical conditions 13, 18

N
National Firearms Licensing Management System 48
notification requirements 25, 58, 85–6

O
ownership, transferring 30, 49, 58, 64, 67, 85–6

P
permits, temporary 39–41
pest control 8–9
pistols 64–6
police
   dealing with 10–11, 23–4, 72
   notifying 25, 39, 58, 85–6
   role of 19–20
possession, age restrictions 53, 57–8
power output 75
prohibited persons 47, 53, 73–4
public places 42, 49, 79–80, 82
purchasing, age restrictions 57–60

R
replacement certificates 39, 61
residency qualifications 22–3
roads, proximity to 36

Royal Society for the Prevention of Cruelty to Animals (RSPCA) 80

S
Scotland 37, 44, 48, 49, 62, 63
Section 7 permits see temporary permits
security of firearms 25, 26, 27–31, 32–5
self-defence 88
serial numbers 15, 85
72-hour rule 86
shot, falling 37–8
shotgun cartridges 88
shotgun certificates (SGC)
   applying for 7, 10
   cartridges 81
   conditions of 32, 44
   drink driving 47–8
   exemptions from 36
   medical conditions 83, 85
   sound moderators 50
   young people 53, 58–60
silencers 50–2
social media 83–4
sound moderators 50–2
storage of firearms 17, 25, 34, 40

T
target hardening 28
target shooting 8, 9, 44, 45, 46–7, 57, 62, 71

temporary accommodation 33–5
temporary permits 39–41, 61
theft of firearms 23
threatening behaviour 17, 74, 88
Town Police Clauses Act 1847 37
transfer of ownership 85–6
transporting guns 32–3
travel 32–5
trespass 49–50

U
unaccompanied possession 44
unannounced visits 19–20

V
vermin 45
violence 74, 88–9
Violent Crime Reduction Act 2006 38
visits, unannounced 19–20

W
Wales 49, 62, 63

Y
young people 52–60

Additional acknowledgements

Images courtesy:
Countrysportimages.com
Nick Ridley
Celine Peniston-Bird
Istockphoto.com/Flowersandclassicalmusic, Martin_33, Photonsage, DemidovSergey, Kadmy and XiXinXing

The British Association for Shooting and Conservation (BASC) is the representative body for country shooting in the UK.

With a membership of over 150,000, BASC is one of the largest field sports organisations in Europe and provides a powerful voice in the public and political arenas for shooting.

With country offices in Scotland, Wales and Northern Ireland, four regional offices in England and its headquarters at Rossett, the association has more than a hundred staff devoted to protecting and promoting shooting sports.

The full-time firearms, gamekeeping, deer, wildfowling and conservation teams are able to give immediate expert advice to members. In one month alone the firearms team will deal with several hundred calls for help from members needing advice, often through difficulties with firearms licensing authorities.

Meanwhile the media and political teams defend our interests among decision makers and in the corridors of power. BASC provides the secretariat for the All-Party Group on Shooting and Conservation at Westminster, ensuring support across the whole political spectrum and providing a direct channel to both government and opposition. With fully-equipped radio and video studios the association provides instant and authoritative comment to the media.

For members there is also unrivalled insurance cover and a wide range of financial benefits. To find out more you can visit www.basc.org.uk or call the membership hotline on 01244 573 030.

Although shooting generally takes place in the countryside, BASC membership reflects the normal distribution of population. This map shows the distribution of BASC members.

Notes